ASVAB Math Practice Workbook

2023

The Most Comprehensive Review for the Math Section of the ASVAB Test

By

Reza Nazari

Copyright © 2023

Effortless Math Education Inc.

All rights reserved. No part of this publication may be reproduced, stored in a retrieval system, or transmitted in any form or by any means, electronic, mechanical, photocopying, recording, scanning, or otherwise, except as permitted under Section 107 or 108 of the 1976 United States Copyright Ac, without permission of the author.

Effortless Math provides unofficial test prep products for a variety of tests and exams. It is not affiliated with or endorsed by any official organizations.

All inquiries should be addressed to:
info@effortlessMath.com
www.EffortlessMath.com

ISBN: 978-1-63719-028-9

Published by: **Effortless Math Education Inc.**

For Online Math Practice Visit www.EffortlessMath.com

Welcome to
ASVAB Math Prep 2023

Thank you for choosing Effortless Math for your ASVAB Math test preparation and congratulations on making the decision to take the ASVAB test! It's a remarkable move you are taking, one that shouldn't be diminished in any capacity.

That's why you need to use every tool possible to ensure you succeed on the test with the highest possible score, and this extensive math workbook is one such tool.

If math has never been a strong subject for you, don't worry! This book along with our online ASVAB Math resources will help you prepare for (and even ACE) the ASVAB Math test. As test day draws nearer, effective preparation becomes increasingly more important. Thankfully, you have this comprehensive workbook to help you get ready for the test. With this book and Effortless Math online resources, you can feel confident that you will be more than ready for the ASVAB Math test when the time comes.

First and foremost, it is important to note that this book is a workbook and not a textbook. Every lesson of this practice book was carefully developed to ensure that you are making the most effective use of your time while preparing for the test. This up-to-date book reflects the 2023 test guidelines and will put you on the right track to hone your math skills, overcome exam anxiety, and boost your confidence, so that you can have your best to succeed on the ASVAB Math test.

This exercise book will:

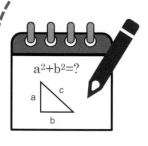

☑ Explain the format of the ASVAB Math test.

☑ Describe specific test-taking strategies that you can use on the test.

☑ Provide ASVAB Math test-taking tips.

☑ Help you identify the areas in which you need to concentrate your study time.

☑ Offer exercises that help you develop the basic math skills you will learn in each section.

☑ Give **2 realistic and full-length practice tests** (featuring new question types) with detailed answers to help you measure your exam readiness and build confidence.

This resource contains comprehensive practice questions and exercises that you will need to prepare for the ASVAB Math test. You'll get numerous skill building exercises as well as tips and techniques on how to prepare for your ASVAB math test.

In addition, in the following pages you'll find:

➢ **How to Use This Book Effectively** – This section provides you with step-by-step instructions on how to get the most out of this comprehensive study guide.

➢ **How to study for the ASVAB Math Test** – A six-step study program has been developed to help you make the best use of this book and prepare for your ASVAB Math test. Here you'll find tips and strategies to guide your study program and help you understand ASVAB Math and how to ace the test.

➢ **ASVAB Math Review** – Learn everything you need to know about the ASVAB Math test.

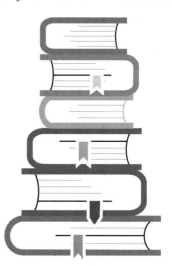

- **ASVAB Math Test-Taking Strategies** – Learn how to effectively put these recommended test-taking techniques into use for improving your ASVAB Math score.

- **Test Day Tips** – Review these tips to make sure you will do your best when the big day comes.

Effortless Math's ASVAB Online Center

Effortless Math Online ASVAB Center offers a complete study program, including the following:

- ✓ Step-by-step instructions on how to prepare for the ASVAB Math test
- ✓ Numerous ASVAB Math worksheets to help you measure your math skills
- ✓ Complete list of ASVAB Math formulas
- ✓ Video lessons for all ASVAB Math topics
- ✓ Full-length ASVAB Math practice tests
- ✓ And much more…

No Registration Required.

Visit **EffortlessMath.com/ASVAB** to find your online ASVAB Math resources.

How to Use This Book Effectively

Look no further when you need a study program to improve your math skills to succeed on the math portion of the ASVAB test. Each chapter of this comprehensive workbook will provide you with the knowledge, tools, and understanding needed for every topic covered on the test.

It's imperative that you understand each topic before moving onto another one, as that's the way to guarantee your success. You can use Effortless Math online course (a free course) to find examples and a step-by-step guide of every math concept in this workbook to better understand the content that will be on the test. To get the best possible results from this book:

- **Begin studying long before your test date.** This provides you ample time to learn the different math concepts. The earlier you begin studying for the test, the sharper your skills will be. Do not procrastinate! Provide yourself with plenty of time to learn the concepts and feel comfortable that you understand them when your test date arrives.
- **Practice consistently.** Study ASVAB Math concepts at least 20 to 30 minutes a day. Remember, slow and steady wins the race, which can be applied to preparing for the ASVAB Math test. Instead of cramming to tackle everything at once, be patient and learn the math topics in short bursts.
- Whenever you get a math problem wrong, **mark it off, and review it later** to make sure you understand the concept.
- Start each session by **looking over the previous material.**
- Once you've reviewed the book's exercises, **take a practice test at the back of the book** to gauge your level of readiness. Then, review your results. Read detailed answers and solutions for each question you missed.
- **Take another practice test** to get an idea of how ready you are to take the actual exam. Taking the practice tests will give you the confidence you need on test day. Simulate the ASVAB testing environment by sitting in a quiet room free from distraction. Make sure to clock yourself with a timer.

How to Study for the ASVAB Math Test

Studying for the ASVAB Math test can be a really daunting and boring task. What's the best way to go about it? Is there a certain study method that works better than others? Well, studying for the ASVAB Math can be done effectively. The following six-step program has been designed to make preparing for the ASVAB Math test more efficient and less overwhelming.

Step 1 - Create a study plan
Step 2 - Choose your study resources
Step 3 - Review, Learn, Practice
Step 4 - Learn and practice test-taking strategies
Step 5 - Learn the ASVAB Test format and take practice tests
Step 6 - Analyze your performance

STEP 1: Create a Study Plan

It's always easier to get things done when you have a plan. Creating a study plan for the ASVAB Math test can help you to stay on track with your studies. It's important to sit down and prepare a study plan with what works with your life, work, and any other obligations you may have. Devote enough time each day to studying. It's also a great idea to break down each section of the exam into blocks and study one concept at a time.

It's important to understand that there is no "right" way to create a study plan. Your study plan will be personalized based on your specific needs and learning style.

Follow these guidelines to create an effective study plan for your ASVAB Math test:

★ **Analyze your learning style and study habits** – Everyone has a different learning style. It is essential to embrace your individuality and the unique way you learn. Think about what works and what doesn't work for you. Do you prefer ASVAB Math prep books or a combination of textbooks and video lessons? Does it work better for you if you study every night for thirty minutes or is it more effective to study in the morning before going to work?

★ **Evaluate your schedule** – Review your current schedule and find out how much time you can consistently devote to ASVAB Math study.

★ **Develop a schedule** – Now it's time to add your study schedule to your calendar like any other obligation. Schedule time for study, practice, and review. Plan out which topic you will study on which day to ensure that you're devoting enough time to each concept. Develop a study plan that is mindful, realistic, and flexible.

★ **Stick to your schedule** – A study plan is only effective when it is followed consistently. You should try to develop a study plan that you can follow for the length of your study program.

★ **Evaluate your study plan and adjust as needed** – Sometimes you need to adjust your plan when you have new commitments. Check in with yourself regularly to make sure that you're not falling behind in your study plan. Remember, the most important thing is sticking to your plan. Your study plan is all about helping you be more productive. If you find that your study plan is not as effective as you want, don't get discouraged. It's okay to make changes as you figure out what works best for you.

STEP 2: Choose Your Study Resources

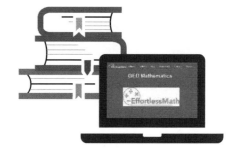

There are numerous textbooks and online resources available for the ASVAB Math test, and it may not be clear where to begin. Don't worry! This exercise book reviews all ASVAB Math concepts and topics. In addition to the book content, you can also use Effortless Math's online resources. (video lessons, worksheets, formulas, etc.) On each page, there is a link (and a QR code) to an online webpage which provides a comprehensive review of the topic, step-by-step instruction, video tutorial, and numerous examples and exercises to help you fully understand the concept.

Simply visit EffortlessMath.com/ASVAB to find your online ASVAB Math resources.

STEP 3: Review, Learn, Practice

This ASVAB Math exercise book breaks down each subject into specific skills or content areas. For instance, the percent concept is separated into different topics—percent calculation, percent increase and decrease, percent problems, etc. Use this book to help you go over all key math concepts and topics on the ASVAB Math test.

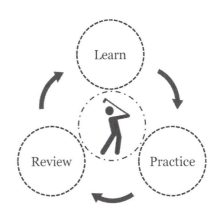

As you review each topic, take notes or highlight the concepts you would like to go over again in the future. If you're unfamiliar with a topic or something is difficult for you, use the link (or the QR code) at the top of the page to find the webpage that provides more instruction about that topic. For each math topic, plenty of instructions, step-by-step guides, and examples are provided to ensure you get a good grasp of the material.

Quickly review the topics you do understand to get a brush-up of the material. Be sure to do the practice questions provided at the end of every chapter to measure your understanding of the concepts.

STEP 4: Learn and Practice Test-taking Strategies

In the following sections, you will find important test-taking strategies and tips that can help you earn extra points. You'll learn how to think strategically and when to guess if you don't know the answer to a question. Using ASVAB Math test-taking strategies and tips can help you raise your score and do well on the test. Apply test taking strategies on the practice tests to help you boost your confidence.

STEP 5: Learn the ASVAB Test Format and Take Practice Tests

The ASVAB *Test Review* section provides information about the structure of the ASVAB test. Read this section to learn more about the ASVAB test structure, different test sections, the number of questions in each section, and the section time limits. When you have a prior understanding of the test format and different types of ASVAB Math questions, you'll feel more confident when you take the actual exam.

Once you have read through the instructions and lessons and feel like you are ready to go – take advantage of both of the full-length ASVAB Math practice tests available in this exercise book. Use the practice tests to sharpen your skills and build confidence.

The ASVAB Math practice tests offered at the end of the book are formatted similarly to the actual ASVAB Math test. When you take each practice test, try to simulate actual testing conditions. To take the practice tests, sit in a quiet space, time yourself, and work through as many of the questions as time allows. The practice tests are followed by detailed answer explanations to help you find your weak areas, learn from your mistakes, and raise your ASVAB Math score.

STEP 6: Analyze Your Performance

After taking the practice tests, look over the answer keys and explanations to learn which questions you answered correctly and which you did not. Never be discouraged if you make a few mistakes. See them as a learning opportunity. This will highlight your strengths and weaknesses.

You can use the results to determine if you need additional practice or if you are ready to take the actual ASVAB Math test.

Looking for more?

Visit EffortlessMath.com/ASVAB to find hundreds of ASVAB Math worksheets, video tutorials, practice tests, ASVAB Math formulas, and much more.

Or scan this QR code.

No Registration Required.

ASVAB Test Review

The Armed Services Vocational Aptitude Battery (ASVAB) was introduced in 1968. Over 40 million examinees have taken the ASVAB since then.

According to official ASVAB website, the ASVAB is a multiple-aptitude battery that measures developed abilities and helps predict future academic and occupational success in the military. It is administered annually to more than one million military applicants, high school, and post-secondary students.

ASVAB scores are reported as percentiles between 1-99. An ASVAB percentile score indicates the percentage of examinees in a reference group that scored at or below that particular score. For example, ASVAB score of 90 indicates that the examinee scored as well as or better than 90% of the nationally-representative sample test takers. An ASVAB score of 60 indicates that the examinee scored as well as or better than 60% of the nationally-representative sample.

There are three types of ASVAB:

- The CAT-ASVAB (computer adaptive test)
- The MET-site ASVAB (paper and pencil (P&P)
- The Student ASVAB (paper and pencil (P&P)

The CAT-ASVAB is a computer adaptive test. It means that if the correct answer is chosen, the next question will be harder. If the answer given is incorrect, the next question will be easier. This also means that once an answer is selected on the CAT it cannot be changed.

The MET- site ASVAB and The Student ASVAB are paper and pencil (P&P) tests.

ASVAB Math Test-Taking Strategies

Here are some test-taking strategies that you can use to maximize your performance and results on the ASVAB Math test.

#1: Use This Approach To Answer Every ASVAB Math Question

- Review the question to identify keywords and important information.
- Translate the keywords into math operations so you can solve the problem.
- Review the answer choices. What are the differences between answer choices?
- Draw or label a diagram if needed.
- Try to find patterns.
- Find the right method to answer the question. Use straightforward math, plug in numbers, or test the answer choices (backsolving).
- Double-check your work.

#2: Use Educated Guessing

This approach is applicable to the problems you understand to some degree but cannot solve using straightforward math. In such cases, try to filter out as many answer choices as possible before picking an answer. In cases where you don't have a clue about what a certain problem entails, don't waste any time trying to eliminate answer choices. Just choose one randomly before moving onto the next question.

As you can ascertain, direct solutions are the most optimal approach. Carefully read through the question, determine what the solution is using the math you have learned before, then coordinate the answer with one of the choices available to you. Are you stumped? Make your best guess, then move on.

Don't leave any fields empty! Even if you're unable to work out a problem, strive to answer it. Take a guess if you have to. You will not lose points by getting an answer wrong, though you may gain a point by getting it correct!

#3: BALLPARK

A ballpark answer is a rough approximation. When we become overwhelmed by calculations and figures, we end up making silly mistakes. A decimal that is moved by one unit can change an answer from right to wrong, regardless of the number of steps that you went through to get it. That's where ballparking can play a big part.

If you think you know what the correct answer may be (even if it's just a ballpark answer), you'll usually have the ability to eliminate a couple of choices. While answer choices are usually based on the average student error and/or values that are closely tied, you will still be able to weed out choices that are way far afield. Try to find answers that aren't in the proverbial ballpark when you're looking for a wrong answer on a multiple-choice question. This is an optimal approach to eliminating answers to a problem.

#4: BACKSOLVING

A majority of questions on the ASVAB Math test will be in multiple-choice format. Many test-takers prefer multiple-choice questions, as at least the answer is right there. You'll typically have four answers to pick from. You simply need to figure out which one is correct. Usually, the best way to go about doing so is "backsolving."

As mentioned earlier, direct solutions are the most optimal approach to answering a question. Carefully read through a problem, calculate a solution, then correspond the answer with one of the choices displayed in front of you. If you can't calculate a solution, your next best approach involves "backsolving."

When backsolving a problem, contrast one of your answer options against the problem you are asked, then see which of them is most relevant. More often than not, answer choices are listed in ascending or descending order. In such cases, try out the choices B or C. If it's not correct, you can go either down or up from there.

#5: Plugging In Numbers

"Plugging in numbers" is a strategy that can be applied to a wide range of different math problems on the ASVAB Math test. This approach is typically used to simplify a challenging question so that it is more understandable. By using the strategy carefully, you can find the answer without too much trouble.

The concept is fairly straightforward–replace unknown variables in a problem with certain values. When selecting a number, consider the following:

- Choose a number that's basic (just not too basic). Generally, you should avoid choosing 1 (or even 0). A decent choice is 2.
- Try not to choose a number that is displayed in the problem.
- Make sure you keep your numbers different if you need to choose at least two of them.
- More often than not, choosing numbers merely lets you filter out some of your answer choices. As such, don't just go with the first choice that gives you the right answer.
- If several answers seem correct, then you'll need to choose another value and try again. This time, though, you'll just need to check choices that haven't been eliminated yet.
- If your question contains fractions, then a potential right answer may involve either an LCD (least common denominator) or an LCD multiple.
- 100 is the number you should choose when you are dealing with problems involving percentages.

ASVAB Math – Test Day Tips

After practicing and reviewing all the math concepts you've been taught, and taking some ASVAB mathematics practice tests, you'll be prepared for test day. Consider the following tips to be extra-ready come test time.

Before Your Test

What to do the night before:

- **Relax!** One day before your test, study lightly or skip studying altogether. You shouldn't attempt to learn something new, either. There are plenty of reasons why studying the evening before a big test can work against you. Put it this way–a marathoner wouldn't go out for a sprint before the day of a big race. Mental marathoners–such as yourself–should not study for any more than one hour 24 hours before a ASVAB test. That's because your brain requires some rest to be at its best. The night before your exam, spend some time with family or friends, or read a book.

- **Avoid bright screens** - You'll have to get some good shuteye the night before your test. Bright screens (such as the ones coming from your laptop, TV, or mobile device) should be avoided altogether. Staring at such a screen will keep your brain up, making it hard to drift asleep at a reasonable hour.

- **Make sure your dinner is healthy** - The meal that you have for dinner should be nutritious. Be sure to drink plenty of water as well. Load up on your complex carbohydrates, much like a marathon runner would do. Pasta, rice, and potatoes are ideal options here, as are vegetables and protein sources.

- **Get your bag ready for test day** - The night prior to your test, pack your bag with your stationery, admissions pass, ID, and any other gear that you need. Keep the bag right by your front door.

- **Make plans to reach the testing site** - Before going to sleep, ensure that you understand precisely how you will arrive at the site of the test. If parking is something you'll have to find first, plan for it. If you're dependent on public transit, then review the schedule. You should also make sure that the train/bus/subway/streetcar you use will be running. Find out about road closures as well. If a parent or friend is accompanying you, ensure that they understand what steps they have to take as well.

The Day of the Test

- **Get up reasonably early, but not too early.**

- **Have breakfast** - Breakfast improves your concentration, memory, and mood. As such, make sure the breakfast that you eat in the morning is healthy. The last thing you want to be is distracted by a grumbling tummy. If it's not your own stomach making those noises, another test taker close to you might be instead. Prevent discomfort or embarrassment by consuming a healthy breakfast. Bring a snack with you if you think you'll need it.

- **Follow your daily routine** - Do you watch Good Morning America each morning while getting ready for the day? Don't break your usual habits on the day of the test. Likewise, if coffee isn't something you drink in the morning, then don't take up the habit hours before your test. Routine consistency lets you concentrate on the main objective–doing the best you can on your test.

- **Wear layers** - Dress yourself up in comfortable layers. You should be ready for any kind of internal temperature. If it gets too warm during the test, take a layer off.

- **Get there on time** - The last thing you want to do is get to the test site late. Rather, you should be there 45 minutes prior to the start of the test. Upon your arrival, try not to hang out with anybody who is nervous. Any anxious energy they exhibit shouldn't influence you.

- **Leave the books at home** - No books should be brought to the test site. If you start developing anxiety before the test, books could encourage you to do some last-minute studying, which will only hinder you. Keep the books far away–better yet, leave them at home.

- **Make your voice heard** - If something is off, speak to a proctor. If medical attention is needed or if you'll require anything, consult the proctor prior to the start of the test. Any doubts you have should be clarified. You should be entering the test site with a state of mind that is completely clear.

- **Have faith in yourself** - When you feel confident, you will be able to perform at your best. When you are waiting for the test to begin, envision yourself receiving an outstanding result. Try to see yourself as someone who knows all the answers, no matter what the questions are. A lot of athletes tend to use this technique–particularly before a big competition. Your expectations will be reflected by your performance.

During your test

- **Be calm and breathe deeply** - You need to relax before the test, and some deep breathing will go a long way to help you do that. Be confident and calm. You got this. Everybody feels a little stressed out just before an evaluation of any kind is set to begin. Learn some effective breathing exercises. Spend a minute meditating before the test starts. Filter out any negative thoughts you have. Exhibit confidence when having such thoughts.

- **Concentrate on the test** - Refrain from comparing yourself to anyone else. You shouldn't be distracted by the people near you or random noise. Concentrate exclusively on the test. If you find yourself irritated by surrounding noises, earplugs can be used to block sounds off close to you. Don't forget–the test is going to last several hours if you're taking more than one subject of the test. Some of that time will be dedicated to brief sections. Concentrate on the specific section you are working on during a particular moment. Do not let your mind wander off to upcoming or previous sections.

- **Try to answer each question individually** - Focus only on the question you are working on. Use one of the test-taking strategies to solve the problem. If you aren't able to come up with an answer, don't get frustrated. Simply skip that question, then move onto the next one.

- **Don't forget to breathe!** Whenever you notice your mind wandering, your stress levels boosting, or frustration brewing, take a thirty-second break. Shut your eyes, drop your pencil, breathe deeply, and let your shoulders relax. You will end up being more productive when you allow yourself to relax for a moment.

- **Optimize your breaks** - When break time comes, use the restroom, have a snack, and reactivate your energy for the subsequent section. Doing some stretches can help stimulate your blood flow.

After your test

- **Take it easy** - You will need to set some time aside to relax and decompress once the test has concluded. There is no need to stress yourself out about what you could've said, or what you may have done wrong. At this point, there's nothing you can do about it. Your energy and time would be better spent on something that will bring you happiness for the remainder of your day.

- **Redoing the test** - Did you pass the test? Congratulations! Your hard work paid off!

If you have failed your test, though, don't worry! The test can be retaken. In such cases, you will need to follow the retake policy. You also need to re-register to take the exam again.

Contents

Chapter 1: Fractions and Mixed Numbers 1
- Simplifying Fractions 2
- Adding and Subtracting Fractions 3
- Multiplying and Dividing Fractions 4
- Adding Mixed Numbers 5
- Subtracting Mixed Numbers 6
- Multiplying Mixed Numbers 7
- Dividing Mixed Numbers 8
- Answers – Chapter 1 9

Chapter 2: Decimal 13
- Comparing Decimals 14
- Rounding Decimals 15
- Adding and Subtracting Decimals 16
- Multiplying and Dividing Decimals 17
- Answers – Chapter 2 18

Chapter 3: Integers and Order of Operations 21
- Adding and Subtracting Integers 22
- Multiplying and Dividing Integers 23
- Order of Operation 24
- Integers and Absolute Value 25
- Answers – Chapter 3 26

Chapter 4: Ratios and Proportions 29
- Simplifying Ratios 30
- Proportional Ratios 31
- Create Proportion 32
- Similarity and Ratios 33
- Simple Interest 34
- Answers – Chapter 4 35

Contents

Chapter 5: Percentage 39
- Percent Problems 40
- Percent of Increase and Decrease 41
- Discount, Tax and Tip 42
- Answers – Chapter 5 43

Chapter 6: Expressions and Variables 45
- Simplifying Variable Expressions 46
- Simplifying Polynomial Expressions 47
- Evaluating One Variable 48
- Evaluating Two Variables 49
- The Distributive Property 50
- Answers – Chapter 6 51

Chapter 7: Equations and Inequalities 55
- One–Step Equations 56
- Multi –Step Equations 57
- System of Equations 58
- Graphing Single–Variable Inequalities 59
- One–Step Inequalities 60
- Multi –Step Inequalities 61
- Answers – Chapter 7 62

Chapter 8: Lines and Slope 67
- Finding Slope 68
- Graphing Lines Using Slope–Intercept Form 69
- Writing Linear Equations 70
- Finding Midpoint 71
- Finding Distance of Two Points 72
- Answers – Chapter 8 73

Chapter 9: Exponents and Variables 77
Multiplication Property of Exponents 78
Division Property of Exponents 79
Powers of Products and Quotients 80
Zero and Negative Exponents 81
Negative Exponents and Negative Bases 82
Scientific Notation 83
Radicals 84
Answers – Chapter 9 85

Chapter 10: Polynomials 91
Simplifying Polynomials 92
Adding and Subtracting Polynomials 93
Multiplying Monomials 94
Multiplying and Dividing Monomials 95
Multiplying a Polynomial and a Monomial 96
Multiplying Binomials 97
Factoring Trinomials 98
Answers – Chapter 10 99

Chapter 11: Geometry and Solid Figures 105
The Pythagorean Theorem 106
Triangles 107
Polygons 108
Circles 109
Cubes 110
Trapezoids 111
Rectangular Prisms 112
Cylinder 113
Answers – Chapter 11 114

Contents

Chapter 12: Statistics 117
    Mean, Median, Mode, and Range of the Given Data 118
    Pie Graph.. 119
    Probability Problems 120
    Permutations and Combinations 121
    Answers – Chapter 12 122

Chapter 13: Functions Operations 125
    Function Notation and Evaluation 126
    Adding and Subtracting Functions 127
    Multiplying and Dividing Functions 128
    Composition of Functions 129
    Answers – Chapter 13 130

Time to Tests.. 132

ASVAB Practice Test 1 133

ASVAB Practice Test 2 149

ASVAB Math Practice Tests Answer Keys 164

ASVAB Practice Tests Answers and Explanations 166

Chapter 1: Fractions and Mixed Numbers

Math Topics that you'll learn in this Chapter:

- ✓ Simplifying Fractions
- ✓ Adding and Subtracting Fractions
- ✓ Multiplying and Dividing Fractions
- ✓ Adding Mixed Numbers
- ✓ Subtracting Mixed Numbers
- ✓ Multiplying Mixed Numbers
- ✓ Dividing Mixed Numbers

Chapter 1: Fractions and Mixed Numbers

Simplifying Fractions

✎ *Simplify each fraction.*

1) $\dfrac{8}{16} =$

2) $\dfrac{7}{21} =$

3) $\dfrac{11}{44} =$

4) $\dfrac{6}{24} =$

5) $\dfrac{6}{18} =$

6) $\dfrac{18}{27} =$

7) $\dfrac{15}{55} =$

8) $\dfrac{24}{54} =$

9) $\dfrac{63}{72} =$

10) $\dfrac{40}{64} =$

11) $\dfrac{23}{46} =$

12) $\dfrac{35}{63} =$

13) $\dfrac{32}{36} =$

14) $\dfrac{81}{99} =$

15) $\dfrac{16}{64} =$

16) $\dfrac{14}{35} =$

17) $\dfrac{19}{38} =$

18) $\dfrac{18}{54} =$

19) $\dfrac{56}{70} =$

20) $\dfrac{40}{45} =$

21) $\dfrac{9}{90} =$

22) $\dfrac{20}{25} =$

23) $\dfrac{36}{42} =$

24) $\dfrac{40}{48} =$

25) $\dfrac{18}{54} =$

26) $\dfrac{48}{144} =$

Chapter 1: Fractions and Mixed Numbers

Adding and Subtracting Fractions

✎ **Calculate and write the answer in lowest term.**

1) $\frac{1}{3} + \frac{1}{5} =$

2) $\frac{2}{5} + \frac{3}{8} =$

3) $\frac{1}{3} - \frac{2}{9} =$

4) $\frac{4}{5} - \frac{2}{9} =$

5) $\frac{2}{9} + \frac{1}{3} =$

6) $\frac{3}{10} + \frac{2}{5} =$

7) $\frac{9}{10} - \frac{4}{5} =$

8) $\frac{7}{9} - \frac{3}{7} =$

9) $\frac{3}{4} + \frac{1}{3} =$

10) $\frac{3}{8} + \frac{2}{5} =$

11) $\frac{3}{4} - \frac{2}{5} =$

12) $\frac{7}{9} - \frac{2}{3} =$

13) $\frac{4}{9} + \frac{5}{6} =$

14) $\frac{2}{3} + \frac{1}{4} =$

15) $\frac{9}{10} - \frac{3}{5} =$

16) $\frac{7}{12} - \frac{1}{2} =$

17) $\frac{4}{5} + \frac{2}{3} =$

18) $\frac{5}{7} + \frac{1}{5} =$

19) $\frac{5}{9} - \frac{2}{5} =$

20) $\frac{3}{5} - \frac{2}{9} =$

21) $\frac{7}{9} + \frac{1}{7} =$

22) $\frac{5}{8} + \frac{2}{3} =$

23) $\frac{5}{7} - \frac{2}{5} =$

24) $\frac{7}{9} - \frac{3}{4} =$

25) $\frac{3}{5} - \frac{1}{6} =$

26) $\frac{3}{12} + \frac{2}{7} =$

Chapter 1: Fractions and Mixed Numbers

Multiplying and Dividing Fractions

✎ Solve and write the answer in lowest term.

1) $\dfrac{1}{3} \times \dfrac{9}{5} =$

2) $\dfrac{1}{4} \times \dfrac{3}{7} =$

3) $\dfrac{1}{5} \div \dfrac{1}{4} =$

4) $\dfrac{1}{6} \div \dfrac{5}{12} =$

5) $\dfrac{2}{3} \times \dfrac{4}{7} =$

6) $\dfrac{5}{7} \times \dfrac{3}{4} =$

7) $\dfrac{2}{5} \div \dfrac{3}{7} =$

8) $\dfrac{3}{7} \div \dfrac{5}{8} =$

9) $\dfrac{3}{8} \times \dfrac{4}{7} =$

10) $\dfrac{2}{9} \times \dfrac{6}{11} =$

11) $\dfrac{1}{10} \div \dfrac{3}{8} =$

12) $\dfrac{3}{10} \div \dfrac{4}{5} =$

13) $\dfrac{6}{7} \times \dfrac{4}{9} =$

14) $\dfrac{3}{7} \times \dfrac{5}{6} =$

15) $\dfrac{7}{9} \div \dfrac{6}{11} =$

16) $\dfrac{1}{15} \div \dfrac{2}{3} =$

17) $\dfrac{1}{13} \times \dfrac{1}{2} =$

18) $\dfrac{1}{12} \times \dfrac{4}{7} =$

19) $\dfrac{1}{15} \div \dfrac{4}{9} =$

20) $\dfrac{1}{16} \div \dfrac{1}{2} =$

21) $\dfrac{4}{7} \times \dfrac{5}{8} =$

22) $\dfrac{1}{11} \times \dfrac{4}{5} =$

23) $\dfrac{1}{16} \div \dfrac{5}{8} =$

24) $\dfrac{1}{15} \div \dfrac{2}{3} =$

25) $\dfrac{1}{13} \times \dfrac{2}{5} =$

26) $\dfrac{1}{18} \times \dfrac{3}{7} =$

Chapter 1: Fractions and Mixed Numbers

Adding Mixed Numbers

✎ *Solve and write the answer in lowest terms.*

1) $1\frac{1}{5} + 2\frac{2}{5} =$

2) $1\frac{1}{2} + 4\frac{5}{6} =$

3) $2\frac{4}{5} + 2\frac{3}{10} =$

4) $3\frac{1}{6} + 2\frac{2}{5} =$

5) $1\frac{5}{6} + 1\frac{2}{5} =$

6) $3\frac{5}{7} + 1\frac{2}{9} =$

7) $3\frac{5}{8} + 2\frac{1}{3} =$

8) $1\frac{6}{7} + 3\frac{2}{9} =$

9) $2\frac{5}{9} + 1\frac{1}{4} =$

10) $3\frac{7}{9} + 2\frac{5}{6} =$

11) $2\frac{1}{10} + 2\frac{2}{5} =$

12) $1\frac{3}{10} + 3\frac{4}{5} =$

13) $3\frac{1}{12} + 2\frac{1}{3} =$

14) $5\frac{1}{11} + 1\frac{1}{2} =$

15) $3\frac{1}{21} + 2\frac{2}{3} =$

16) $4\frac{1}{24} + 1\frac{5}{8} =$

17) $2\frac{1}{25} + 3\frac{3}{5} =$

18) $3\frac{1}{15} + 2\frac{2}{10} =$

19) $5\frac{6}{7} + 2\frac{1}{3} =$

20) $2\frac{1}{8} + 3\frac{3}{4} =$

21) $2\frac{5}{7} + 2\frac{2}{21} =$

22) $4\frac{1}{6} + 1\frac{4}{5} =$

23) $2\frac{1}{7} + 2\frac{3}{8} =$

24) $3\frac{1}{4} + 2\frac{2}{3} =$

25) $1\frac{1}{13} + 2\frac{3}{4} =$

26) $3\frac{2}{35} + 2\frac{5}{7} =$

Chapter 1: Fractions and Mixed Numbers

Subtracting Mixed Numbers

✏️ *Solve and write the answer in lowest terms.*

1) $5\frac{2}{9} - 2\frac{1}{9} =$

2) $6\frac{2}{7} - 2\frac{1}{3} =$

3) $5\frac{3}{8} - 2\frac{3}{4} =$

4) $7\frac{2}{5} - 3\frac{1}{10} =$

5) $9\frac{5}{7} - 7\frac{4}{21} =$

6) $11\frac{7}{12} - 9\frac{5}{6} =$

7) $9\frac{5}{9} - 8\frac{1}{8} =$

8) $13\frac{7}{9} - 11\frac{3}{7} =$

9) $8\frac{7}{12} - 7\frac{3}{8} =$

10) $11\frac{5}{9} - 9\frac{1}{4} =$

11) $6\frac{5}{6} - 2\frac{2}{9} =$

12) $5\frac{7}{8} - 4\frac{1}{3} =$

13) $9\frac{5}{8} - 8\frac{1}{2} =$

14) $4\frac{9}{16} - 2\frac{1}{4} =$

15) $3\frac{2}{3} - 1\frac{2}{15} =$

16) $5\frac{1}{2} - 4\frac{2}{17} =$

17) $5\frac{6}{7} - 2\frac{1}{3} =$

18) $3\frac{3}{7} - 2\frac{2}{21} =$

19) $7\frac{3}{10} - 5\frac{2}{15} =$

20) $4\frac{5}{6} - 2\frac{2}{9} =$

21) $6\frac{3}{7} - 2\frac{2}{9} =$

22) $7\frac{4}{5} - 6\frac{3}{7} =$

23) $12\frac{3}{7} - 8\frac{1}{3} =$

24) $5\frac{4}{9} - 2\frac{5}{6} =$

25) $10\frac{1}{28} - 7\frac{3}{4} =$

26) $11\frac{5}{12} - 7\frac{5}{48} =$

Chapter 1: Fractions and Mixed Numbers

Multiplying Mixed Numbers

✍ **Solve and write the answer in lowest terms.**

1) $1\frac{1}{6} \times 1\frac{3}{7} =$

2) $5\frac{1}{6} \times 2\frac{1}{4} =$

3) $3\frac{3}{7} \times 1\frac{2}{9} =$

4) $3\frac{3}{8} \times 3\frac{1}{6} =$

5) $1\frac{1}{2} \times 5\frac{2}{3} =$

6) $3\frac{1}{2} \times 6\frac{2}{3} =$

7) $9\frac{1}{2} \times 2\frac{1}{6} =$

8) $2\frac{5}{8} \times 8\frac{3}{5} =$

9) $3\frac{4}{5} \times 4\frac{2}{3} =$

10) $5\frac{1}{3} \times 2\frac{2}{7} =$

11) $6\frac{1}{3} \times 3\frac{3}{4} =$

12) $7\frac{2}{3} \times 1\frac{8}{9} =$

13) $8\frac{1}{2} \times 2\frac{1}{6} =$

14) $4\frac{1}{5} \times 8\frac{2}{3} =$

15) $3\frac{1}{8} \times 5\frac{2}{3} =$

16) $2\frac{2}{7} \times 6\frac{2}{5} =$

17) $2\frac{3}{8} \times 7\frac{2}{3} =$

18) $1\frac{7}{8} \times 8\frac{2}{3} =$

19) $9\frac{1}{2} \times 3\frac{1}{5} =$

20) $2\frac{5}{8} \times 4\frac{1}{3} =$

21) $6\frac{1}{3} \times 3\frac{2}{5} =$

22) $5\frac{3}{4} \times 2\frac{2}{7} =$

23) $8\frac{1}{6} \times 2\frac{2}{7} =$

24) $4\frac{1}{6} \times 7\frac{1}{5} =$

25) $2\frac{1}{5} \times 2\frac{5}{8} =$

26) $6\frac{2}{3} \times 4\frac{3}{5} =$

Chapter 1: Fractions and Mixed Numbers

Dividing Mixed Numbers

Solve and write the answer in lowest terms.

1) $6\frac{1}{2} \div 4\frac{2}{5} =$

2) $1\frac{3}{8} \div 1\frac{1}{4} =$

3) $6\frac{2}{5} \div 2\frac{4}{5} =$

4) $7\frac{1}{3} \div 6\frac{3}{4} =$

5) $7\frac{2}{5} \div 3\frac{3}{4} =$

6) $2\frac{4}{5} \div 3\frac{2}{3} =$

7) $8\frac{3}{5} \div 4\frac{3}{4} =$

8) $6\frac{3}{4} \div 2\frac{2}{9} =$

9) $5\frac{2}{7} \div 2\frac{2}{9} =$

10) $2\frac{2}{5} \div 3\frac{3}{5} =$

11) $4\frac{3}{7} \div 1\frac{7}{8} =$

12) $2\frac{5}{7} \div 2\frac{4}{5} =$

13) $8\frac{3}{5} \div 6\frac{1}{5} =$

14) $2\frac{5}{8} \div 1\frac{8}{9} =$

15) $5\frac{6}{7} \div 2\frac{3}{4} =$

16) $1\frac{3}{5} \div 2\frac{3}{8} =$

17) $5\frac{3}{4} \div 3\frac{2}{5} =$

18) $2\frac{3}{4} \div 3\frac{1}{5} =$

19) $3\frac{2}{3} \div 1\frac{2}{5} =$

20) $4\frac{1}{4} \div 2\frac{2}{3} =$

21) $3\frac{5}{6} \div 2\frac{4}{5} =$

22) $2\frac{1}{8} \div 1\frac{3}{4} =$

23) $5\frac{1}{2} \div 4\frac{2}{5} =$

24) $6\frac{3}{7} \div 2\frac{1}{7} =$

25) $3\frac{3}{6} \div 1\frac{5}{7} =$

26) $4\frac{4}{9} \div 4\frac{2}{3} =$

Chapter 1: Fractions and Mixed Numbers

Answers – Chapter 1

Simplifying Fractions

1) $\dfrac{1}{2}$ 8) $\dfrac{4}{9}$ 15) $\dfrac{1}{4}$ 22) $\dfrac{4}{5}$

2) $\dfrac{1}{3}$ 9) $\dfrac{7}{8}$ 16) $\dfrac{2}{5}$ 23) $\dfrac{6}{7}$

3) $\dfrac{1}{4}$ 10) $\dfrac{5}{8}$ 17) $\dfrac{1}{2}$ 24) $\dfrac{5}{6}$

4) $\dfrac{1}{4}$ 11) $\dfrac{1}{2}$ 18) $\dfrac{1}{3}$ 25) $\dfrac{1}{3}$

5) $\dfrac{1}{3}$ 12) $\dfrac{5}{9}$ 19) $\dfrac{4}{5}$ 26) $\dfrac{1}{3}$

6) $\dfrac{2}{3}$ 13) $\dfrac{8}{9}$ 20) $\dfrac{8}{9}$

7) $\dfrac{3}{11}$ 14) $\dfrac{9}{11}$ 21) $\dfrac{1}{10}$

Adding and Subtracting Fractions

1) $\dfrac{8}{15}$ 8) $\dfrac{22}{63}$ 15) $\dfrac{3}{10}$ 22) $\dfrac{31}{24}$

2) $\dfrac{31}{40}$ 9) $\dfrac{13}{12}$ 16) $\dfrac{1}{12}$ 23) $\dfrac{11}{35}$

3) $\dfrac{1}{9}$ 10) $\dfrac{31}{40}$ 17) $\dfrac{22}{15}$ 24) $\dfrac{1}{36}$

4) $\dfrac{26}{45}$ 11) $\dfrac{7}{20}$ 18) $\dfrac{32}{35}$ 25) $\dfrac{13}{30}$

5) $\dfrac{5}{9}$ 12) $\dfrac{1}{9}$ 19) $\dfrac{7}{45}$ 26) $\dfrac{15}{28}$

6) $\dfrac{7}{10}$ 13) $\dfrac{23}{18}$ 20) $\dfrac{17}{45}$

7) $\dfrac{1}{10}$ 14) $\dfrac{11}{12}$ 21) $\dfrac{58}{63}$

Chapter 1: Fractions and Mixed Numbers

Multiplying and Dividing Fractions

1) $\frac{3}{5}$
2) $\frac{3}{28}$
3) $\frac{4}{5}$
4) $\frac{2}{5}$
5) $\frac{8}{21}$
6) $\frac{15}{28}$
7) $\frac{14}{15}$
8) $\frac{24}{35}$
9) $\frac{3}{14}$
10) $\frac{4}{33}$
11) $\frac{4}{15}$
12) $\frac{3}{8}$
13) $\frac{8}{21}$
14) $\frac{5}{14}$
15) $\frac{77}{54}$
16) $\frac{1}{10}$
17) $\frac{1}{26}$
18) $\frac{1}{21}$
19) $\frac{3}{20}$
20) $\frac{1}{8}$
21) $\frac{5}{14}$
22) $\frac{4}{55}$
23) $\frac{1}{10}$
24) $\frac{1}{10}$
25) $\frac{2}{65}$
26) $\frac{1}{42}$

Adding Mixed Numbers

1) $3\frac{3}{5}$
2) $6\frac{1}{3}$
3) $5\frac{1}{10}$
4) $5\frac{17}{30}$
5) $3\frac{7}{30}$
6) $4\frac{59}{63}$
7) $5\frac{23}{24}$
8) $5\frac{5}{63}$
9) $3\frac{29}{36}$
10) $6\frac{11}{18}$
11) $4\frac{1}{2}$
12) $5\frac{1}{10}$
13) $5\frac{5}{12}$
14) $6\frac{13}{22}$
15) $5\frac{5}{7}$
16) $5\frac{2}{3}$
17) $5\frac{16}{25}$
18) $5\frac{4}{15}$
19) $8\frac{4}{21}$
20) $5\frac{7}{8}$
21) $4\frac{17}{21}$
22) $5\frac{29}{30}$
23) $4\frac{29}{56}$
24) $5\frac{11}{12}$
25) $3\frac{43}{52}$
26) $5\frac{27}{35}$

Chapter 1: Fractions and Mixed Numbers

Subtracting Mixed Numbers

1) $3\frac{1}{9}$
2) $3\frac{20}{21}$
3) $2\frac{5}{8}$
4) $4\frac{3}{10}$
5) $2\frac{11}{21}$
6) $1\frac{3}{4}$
7) $1\frac{31}{72}$
8) $2\frac{22}{63}$
9) $1\frac{5}{24}$
10) $2\frac{11}{36}$
11) $4\frac{11}{18}$
12) $1\frac{13}{24}$
13) $1\frac{1}{8}$
14) $2\frac{5}{16}$
15) $2\frac{8}{15}$
16) $1\frac{13}{34}$
17) $3\frac{11}{21}$
18) $1\frac{1}{3}$
19) $2\frac{1}{6}$
20) $2\frac{11}{18}$
21) $4\frac{13}{63}$
22) $1\frac{13}{35}$
23) $4\frac{2}{21}$
24) $2\frac{11}{18}$
25) $2\frac{2}{7}$
26) $4\frac{5}{16}$

Multiplying Mixed Numbers

1) $1\frac{2}{3}$
2) $11\frac{5}{8}$
3) $4\frac{4}{21}$
4) $10\frac{11}{16}$
5) $8\frac{1}{2}$
6) $23\frac{1}{3}$
7) $20\frac{7}{12}$
8) $22\frac{23}{40}$
9) $17\frac{11}{15}$
10) $12\frac{4}{21}$
11) $23\frac{3}{4}$
12) $14\frac{13}{27}$
13) $18\frac{5}{12}$
14) $36\frac{2}{5}$
15) $17\frac{17}{24}$
16) $14\frac{22}{35}$
17) $18\frac{5}{24}$
18) $16\frac{1}{4}$
19) $30\frac{2}{5}$
20) $11\frac{3}{8}$
21) $21\frac{8}{15}$
22) $13\frac{1}{7}$
23) $18\frac{2}{3}$
24) 30
25) $5\frac{31}{40}$
26) $30\frac{2}{3}$

Chapter 1: Fractions and Mixed Numbers

Dividing Mixed Numbers

1) $1\frac{21}{44}$

2) $1\frac{1}{10}$

3) $2\frac{2}{7}$

4) $1\frac{7}{81}$

5) $1\frac{73}{75}$

6) $\frac{42}{55}$

7) $1\frac{77}{95}$

8) $3\frac{3}{80}$

9) $2\frac{53}{140}$

10) $\frac{2}{3}$

11) $2\frac{88}{105}$

12) $\frac{95}{98}$

13) $1\frac{12}{31}$

14) $1\frac{53}{136}$

15) $2\frac{10}{77}$

16) $\frac{64}{95}$

17) $1\frac{47}{68}$

18) $\frac{55}{64}$

19) $2\frac{13}{21}$

20) $1\frac{19}{32}$

21) $1\frac{31}{84}$

22) $1\frac{3}{14}$

23) $1\frac{1}{4}$

24) 3

25) $2\frac{1}{24}$

26) $\frac{20}{21}$

Chapter 2: Decimal

Math Topics that you'll learn in this Chapter:

- ✓ Comparing Decimals
- ✓ Rounding Decimals
- ✓ Adding and Subtracting Decimals
- ✓ Multiplying and Dividing Decimals

Chapter 2: Decimal

Comparing Decimals

✏️ **Compare. Use >, =, and <**

1) 0.44 ☐ 0.044
2) 0.67 ☐ 0.68
3) 0.49 ☐ 0.79
4) 1.35 ☐ 1.45
5) 1.58 ☐ 1.75
6) 2.91 ☐ 2.85
7) 14.56 ☐ 1.456
8) 17.85 ☐ 17.89
9) 21.52 ☐ 21.052
10) 11.12 ☐ 11.03
11) 9.650 ☐ 9.65
12) 8.578 ☐ 8.568
13) 3.15 ☐ 0.315
14) 16.61 ☐ 16.16
15) 18.581 ☐ 8.991
16) 25.05 ☐ 2.505

17) 4.55 ☐ 4.65
18) 0.158 ☐ 1.58
19) 0.881 ☐ 0.871
20) 0.505 ☐ 0.510
21) 0.772 ☐ 0.777
22) 0.5 ☐ 0.500
23) 16.89 ☐ 15.89
24) 12.25 ☐ 12.35
25) 5.82 ☐ 5.69
26) 1.320 ☐ 1.032
27) 0.082 ☐ 0.088
28) 0.99 ☐ 0.099
29) 2.360 ☐ 2.840
30) 0.330 ☐ 0.303
31) 16.44 ☐ 1.664
32) 0.424 ☐ 0.442

Chapter 2: Decimal

Rounding Decimals

Round each number to the underlined place value.

1) 3.960 =

2) 4.3_7_2 =

3) 11.1_3_6 =

4) 1_7_.5 =

5) 1.9_8_1 =

6) 14._2_15 =

7) 17.5_4_8 =

8) 25.5_0_8 =

9) 3_1_.089 =

10) 69._3_45 =

11) 9.4_5_7 =

12) 1_2_.901 =

13) 2.6_5_8 =

14) 32._5_65 =

15) 6.0_5_8 =

16) 98.1_0_8 =

17) 27._7_05 =

18) 3_6_.75 =

19) 9._0_8 =

20) 7.1_8_5 =

21) 22.5_4_7 =

22) 66._0_98 =

23) 8_7_.75 =

24) 18._5_41 =

25) 10.2_5_8 =

26) 13._4_56 =

27) 71.0_8_4 =

28) 2_9_.23 =

29) 43._4_5 =

30) 8_1_.07 =

31) 9_2_.366 =

32) 24._7_6 =

Chapter 2: Decimal

Adding and Subtracting Decimals

✏ **Solve.**

1) $11.62 + 18.23 =$

2) $13.78 + 16.58 =$

3) $56.30 - 45.68 =$

4) $59.36 - 30.88 =$

5) $24.32 + 26.45 =$

6) $36.25 + 18.37 =$

7) $47.85 - 35.12 =$

8) $85.65 - 67.48 =$

9) $25.49 + 34.18 =$

10) $19.99 + 48.66 =$

11) $46.32 - 27.77 =$

12) $54.62 - 48.12 =$

13) $24.42 + 16.54 =$

14) $52.13 + 12.32 =$

15) $82.36 - 78.65 =$

16) $64.12 - 49.15 =$

17) $36.41 + 24.52 =$

18) $85.96 - 74.63 =$

19) $52.62 - 42.54 =$

20) $21.20 + 24.58 =$

21) $32.15 + 17.17 =$

22) $96.32 - 85.54 =$

23) $89.78 - 69.85 =$

24) $29.28 + 39.79 =$

25) $11.11 + 19.99 =$

26) $28.82 + 20.88 =$

27) $63.14 - 28.91 =$

28) $56.61 - 49.72 =$

29) $66.14 + 32.12 =$

30) $30.19 + 25.83 =$

31) $68.21 - 25.10 =$

32) $76.57 - 45.13 =$

Chapter 2: Decimal

Multiplying and Dividing Decimals

Solve.

1) $12.3 \times 0.2 =$

2) $12.6 \times 0.9 =$

3) $54.4 \div 2 =$

4) $64.8 \div 8 =$

5) $23.1 \times 0.3 =$

6) $1.2 \times 0.7 =$

7) $5.5 \div 0.5 =$

8) $64.8 \div 8 =$

9) $1.4 \times 0.5 =$

10) $4.5 \times 0.3 =$

11) $88.8 \div 4 =$

12) $10.5 \div 5 =$

13) $2.2 \times 0.3 =$

14) $0.2 \times 0.52 =$

15) $95.7 \div 100 =$

16) $36.6 \div 6 =$

17) $3.2 \times 2 =$

18) $4.1 \times 0.5 =$

19) $68.4 \div 2 =$

20) $27.9 \div 9 =$

21) $3.5 \times 4 =$

22) $4.8 \times 0.5 =$

23) $6.4 \div 4 =$

24) $72.8 \div 0.8 =$

25) $1.8 \times 3 =$

26) $6.5 \times 0.2 =$

27) $93.6 \div 3 =$

28) $45.15 \div 0.5 =$

29) $12.6 \times 0.5 =$

30) $13.2 \times 6 =$

31) $6.4 \div 0.8 =$

32) $98.6 \div 0.2 =$

Chapter 2: Decimal

Answers – Chapter 2

Comparing Decimals

1) 0.44 > 0.044

2) 0.67 < 0.68

3) 0.49 < 0.79

4) 1.35 < 1.45

5) 1.58 < 1.75

6) 2.91 > 2.85

7) 14.56 > 1.456

8) 17.85 < 17.89

9) 21.52 > 21.052

10) 11.12 > 11.03

11) 9.650 = 9.65

12) 8.578 > 8.568

13) 3.15 > 0.315

14) 16.61 > 16.16

15) 18.581 > 8.991

16) 25.05 > 2.505

17) 4.55 < 4.65

18) 0.158 < 1.58

19) 0.881 > 0.871

20) 0.505 < 0.510

21) 0.772 < 0.777

22) 0.5 = 0.500

23) 16.89 > 15.89

24) 12.25 < 12.35

25) 5.82 > 5.69

26) 1.320 > 1.032

27) 0.082 < 0.088

28) 0.99 > 0.099

29) 2.360 < 2.840

30) 0.330 > 0.303

31) 16.44 > 1.664

32) 0.424 < 0.442

Chapter 2: Decimal

Rounding Decimals

1) 3.960 = 4

2) 4.372 = 4.37

3) 11.136 = 11.14

4) 17.5 = 18

5) 1.981 = 1.98

6) 14.215 = 14.2

7) 17.548 = 17.55

8) 25.508 = 25.51

9) 31.089 = 31

10) 69.345 = 69.3

11) 9.457 = 9.46

12) 12.901 = 13

13) 2.658 = 2.66

14) 32.565 = 32.6

15) 6.058 = 6.06

16) 98.108 = 98.11

17) 27.705 = 27.7

18) 36.75 = 37

19) 9.08 = 9.1

20) 7.185 = 7.2

21) 22.547 = 22.55

22) 66.098 = 66.1

23) 87.75 = 88

24) 18.541 = 18.5

25) 10.258 = 10.26

26) 13.456 = 13.5

27) 71.084 = 71.08

28) 29.23 = 29

29) 43.45 = 43.5

30) 81.07 = 81

31) 92.366 = 92

32) 24.76 = 24.8

Chapter 2: Decimal

Adding and Subtracting Decimals

1) 29.85
2) 30.36
3) 10.62
4) 28.48
5) 50.77
6) 54.62
7) 12.73
8) 18.17
9) 59.67
10) 68.65
11) 18.55
12) 6.5
13) 40.96
14) 64.45
15) 3.71
16) 14.97
17) 60.93
18) 11.33
19) 10.08
20) 45.78
21) 49.32
22) 10.78
23) 19.93
24) 69.07
25) 31.1
26) 49.7
27) 34.23
28) 6.89
29) 98.26
30) 56.02
31) 43.11
32) 31.44

Multiplying and Dividing Decimals

1) 2.46
2) 11.34
3) 27.2
4) 8.1
5) 6.93
6) 0.84
7) 11
8) 8.1
9) 0.7
10) 1.35
11) 22.2
12) 2.1
13) 0.66
14) 0.104
15) 0.957
16) 6.1
17) 6.4
18) 2.05
19) 34.2
20) 3.1
21) 14
22) 2.4
23) 1.6
24) 91
25) 5.4
26) 1.3
27) 31.2
28) 90.3
29) 6.3
30) 79.2
31) 8
32) 493

Chapter 3: Integers and Order of Operations

Math Topics that you'll learn in this Chapter:

- ✓ Adding and Subtracting Integers
- ✓ Multiplying and Dividing Integers
- ✓ Order of Operations
- ✓ Integers and Absolute Value

Chapter 3: Integers and Order of Operations

Adding and Subtracting Integers

Solve.

1) $-(9) + 15 =$

2) $15 - (-11 - 9) =$

3) $(-10) + (-6) =$

4) $(-10) + (-6) + 7 =$

5) $-(23) + 19 =$

6) $(-7 + 5) - 9 =$

7) $28 + (-32) =$

8) $(-11) + (-9) + 5 =$

9) $25 - (8 - 7) =$

10) $-(29) + 17 =$

11) $(-38) + (-3) + 29 =$

12) $15 - (-7 + 9) =$

13) $24 - (8 - 2) =$

14) $(-7 + 4) - 9 =$

15) $(-17) + (-3) + 9 =$

16) $(-26) + (-7) + 8 =$

17) $(-9) + (-11) =$

18) $8 - (-23 - 13) =$

19) $(-16) + (-2) =$

20) $25 - (7 - 4) =$

21) $23 + (-12) =$

22) $(-18) + (-6) =$

23) $17 - (-21 - 7) =$

24) $-(28) - (-16) + 5 =$

25) $(-9 + 4) - 8 =$

26) $(-28) + (-6) + 17 =$

27) $-(21) - (-15) + 9 =$

28) $(-31) + (-6) =$

29) $(-18) + (-10) + 13 =$

30) $(-30) + (-11) + 12 =$

31) $-(28) - (-10) + 6 =$

32) $6 - (-16 - 11) =$

Chapter 3: Integers and Order of Operations

Multiplying and Dividing Integers

Solve.

1) $(-6) \times (-7) =$

2) $8 \times (-5) =$

3) $48 \div (-8) =$

4) $(-72) \div 9 =$

5) $(4) \times (-6) =$

6) $(-9) \times (-11) =$

7) $(10) \div (-5) =$

8) $144 \div (-12) =$

9) $(10) \times (-2) =$

10) $(-8) \times (-2) \times 5 =$

11) $(8) \div (-2) =$

12) $45 \div (-15) =$

13) $(5) \times (-7) =$

14) $(-6) \times (-5) \times 4 =$

15) $(12) \div (-6) =$

16) $(14) \div (-7) =$

17) $196 \div (-14) =$

18) $(27 - 13) \times (-2) =$

19) $125 \div (-5) =$

20) $66 \div (-6) =$

21) $(-6) \times (-5) \times 3 =$

22) $(15 - 6) \times (-3) =$

23) $(32 - 24) \div (-4) =$

24) $72 \div (-6) =$

25) $(-14 + 8) \times (-7) =$

26) $(-3) \times (-9) \times 3 =$

27) $84 \div (-12) =$

28) $(-12) \times (-10) =$

29) $22 \times (-3) =$

30) $(-2) \times (-6) \times 5 =$

31) $(24) \div (-3) =$

32) $(-15) \div (3) =$

Chapter 3: Integers and Order of Operations

Order of Operation

✎ Calculate.

1) $16 + (30 ÷ 5) =$

2) $(3 × 9) ÷ (−3) =$

3) $57 − (3 × 8) =$

4) $(−12) × (7 − 3) =$

5) $(18 − 7) × (6) =$

6) $(6 × 10) ÷ (12 + 3) =$

7) $(13 × 2) − (24 ÷ 6) =$

8) $(−5) + (4 × 3) + 8 =$

9) $(4 × 2^3) + (16 − 9) =$

10) $(3^2 × 7) ÷ (−2 + 1) =$

11) $[−2(48 ÷ 2^3)] − 6 =$

12) $(−4) + (7 × 8) + 18 =$

13) $(3 × 7) + (16 − 7) =$

14) $[3^3 × (48 ÷ 2^3)] ÷ (−2) =$

15) $(14 × 3) − (3^4 ÷ 9) =$

16) $(96 ÷ 12) × (−3) =$

17) $(48 ÷ 2^2) × (−2) =$

18) $(56 ÷ 7) × (−5) =$

19) $(−2^2) + (7 × 9) − 21 =$

20) $(2^4 − 9) × (−6) =$

21) $[4^3 × (50 ÷ 5^2)] ÷ (−16) =$

22) $(3^2 × 4^2) ÷ (−4 + 2) =$

23) $6^2 − (−6 × 4) + 3 =$

24) $4^2 − (5^2 × 3) =$

25) $(−4) + (12^2 ÷ 3^2) − 7^2 =$

26) $(3^2 × 5) + (−5^2 − 9) =$

27) $2[(3^2 × 5) × (−6)] =$

28) $(11^2 − 2^2) − (−7^2) =$

29) $(2^2 × 5) − (64 ÷ 8) =$

30) $2[(3^2 × 4) + (35 ÷ 5)] =$

31) $(4^2 × 3) ÷ (−6) =$

32) $3^2[(4^3 ÷ 16) − (3^3 ÷ 27)] =$

Chapter 3: Integers and Order of Operations

Integers and Absolute Value

Calculate.

1) $4 - |6 - 10| =$

2) $|14| - \frac{|-18|}{3} =$

3) $\frac{|8 \times -8|}{4} \times \frac{|-20|}{5} =$

4) $|12 \times 3| + \frac{|-81|}{9} =$

5) $4 - |11 - 18| - |3| =$

6) $|18| - \frac{|-12|}{4} =$

7) $\frac{|5 \times -8|}{10} \times \frac{|-22|}{11} =$

8) $|9 \times 3| + \frac{|-36|}{4} =$

9) $|-42 + 7| \times \frac{|-2 \times 5|}{10} =$

10) $6 - |17 - 11| - |5| =$

11) $|13| - \frac{|-54|}{6} =$

12) $\frac{|9 \times -4|}{12} \times \frac{|-45|}{9} =$

13) $|-75 + 50| \times \frac{|-4 \times 5|}{5} =$

14) $\frac{|-26|}{13} \times \frac{|-32|}{8} =$

15) $14 - |8 - 18| - |-12| =$

16) $|29| - \frac{|-20|}{5} =$

17) $\frac{|3 \times 8|}{2} \times \frac{|-33|}{3} =$

18) $|-45 + 15| \times \frac{|-12 \times 5|}{6} =$

19) $\frac{|-50|}{5} \times \frac{|-77|}{11} =$

20) $12 - |2 - 7| - |15| =$

21) $|18| - \frac{|-45|}{15} =$

22) $\frac{|7 \times 8|}{4} \times \frac{|-48|}{12} =$

23) $\frac{|30 \times 2|}{3} \times |-12| =$

24) $\frac{|-36|}{9} \times \frac{|-80|}{8} =$

25) $|-30 + 9| \times \frac{|-8 \times 5|}{8} =$

26) $|16| - \frac{|-18|}{3} =$

27) $12 - |10 - 24| + |5| =$

28) $|-38 + 8| \times \frac{|-5 \times 6|}{10} =$

Chapter 3: Integers and Order of Operations

Answers – Chapter 3

Adding and Subtracting Integers

1) 6
2) 35
3) −16
4) −9
5) −4
6) −11
7) −4
8) −15
9) 24
10) −12
11) −12
12) 13
13) 18
14) −12
15) −11
16) −25
17) −20
18) 44
19) −18
20) 22
21) 11
22) −24
23) 45
24) −7
25) −13
26) −17
27) 3
28) −37
29) −15
30) −29
31) −12
32) 33

Multiplying and Dividing Integers

1) 42
2) −40
3) −6
4) −8
5) −24
6) 99
7) −2
8) −12
9) −20
10) 80
11) −4
12) −3
13) −35
14) 120
15) −2
16) −2
17) −14
18) −28
19) −25
20) −11
21) 90
22) −27
23) −2
24) −12
25) 42
26) 81
27) −7
28) 120
29) −66
30) 60
31) −8
32) −5

www.EffortlessMath.com

Chapter 3: Integers and Order of Operations

Order of Operation

1) 22	9) 39	17) −24	25) −37
2) −9	10) −63	18) −40	26) 11
3) 33	11) −18	19) 38	27) −540
4) −48	12) 70	20) −42	28) 166
5) 66	13) 30	21) −8	29) 12
6) 4	14) −81	22) −72	30) 86
7) 22	15) 33	23) 63	31) −8
8) 15	16) −24	24) −59	32) 27

Integers and Absolute Value

1) 0	8) 36	15) −8	22) 56
2) 8	9) 35	16) 25	23) 240
3) 64	10) −5	17) 132	24) 40
4) 45	11) 4	18) 300	25) 105
5) −6	12) 15	19) 70	26) 10
6) 15	13) 100	20) −8	27) 3
7) 8	14) 8	21) 15	28) 90

Chapter 4: Ratios and Proportions

Math Topics that you'll learn in this Chapter:

- ✓ Simplifying Ratios
- ✓ Proportional Ratios
- ✓ Similarity and Ratios
- ✓ Simple Interest

Chapter 4: Ratios and Proportions

Simplifying Ratios

Simplify each ratio.

1) $3:21 =$ ___ : ___

2) $4:16 =$ ___ : ___

3) $\dfrac{2}{28} = -$

4) $\dfrac{18}{45} = -$

5) $10:30 =$ ___ : ___

6) $5:30 =$ ___ : ___

7) $\dfrac{34}{38} = -$

8) $\dfrac{45}{63} = -$

9) $10:45 =$ ___ : ___

10) $20:30 =$ ___ : ___

11) $\dfrac{40}{64} = -$

12) $\dfrac{10}{110} = -$

13) $8:12 =$ ___ : ___

14) $16:20 =$ ___ : ___

15) $\dfrac{24}{48} = -$

16) $\dfrac{21}{77} = -$

17) $8:24 =$ ___ : ___

18) $9 \text{ to } 36 =$ ___ : ___

19) $\dfrac{64}{72} = -$

20) $\dfrac{45}{60} = -$

21) $12:15 =$ ___ : ___

22) $18:54 =$ ___ : ___

23) $\dfrac{36}{54} = -$

24) $\dfrac{48}{104} = -$

25) $12:48 =$ ___ : ___

26) $18:72 =$ ___ : ___

27) $\dfrac{15}{75} = -$

28) $\dfrac{46}{52} = -$

Chapter 4: Ratios and Proportions

Proportional Ratios

Solve each proportion for x.

1) $\frac{4}{7} = \frac{8}{x}$, $x =$ _____

2) $\frac{9}{12} = \frac{x}{8}$, $x =$ _____

3) $\frac{3}{5} = \frac{12}{x}$, $x =$ _____

4) $\frac{3}{10} = \frac{x}{50}$, $x =$ _____

5) $\frac{3}{11} = \frac{15}{x}$, $x =$ _____

6) $\frac{6}{15} = \frac{x}{45}$, $x =$ _____

7) $\frac{6}{19} = \frac{12}{x}$, $x =$ _____

8) $\frac{7}{16} = \frac{x}{32}$, $x =$ _____

9) $\frac{18}{21} = \frac{54}{x}$, $x =$ _____

10) $\frac{13}{15} = \frac{39}{x}$, $x =$ _____

11) $\frac{9}{13} = \frac{72}{x}$, $x =$ _____

12) $\frac{8}{30} = \frac{x}{180}$, $x =$ _____

13) $\frac{3}{19} = \frac{9}{x}$, $x =$ _____

14) $\frac{1}{3} = \frac{x}{90}$, $x =$ _____

15) $\frac{25}{45} = \frac{x}{9}$, $x =$ _____

16) $\frac{1}{6} = \frac{9}{x}$, $x =$ _____

17) $\frac{7}{9} = \frac{63}{x}$, $x =$ _____

18) $\frac{54}{72} = \frac{x}{8}$, $x =$ _____

19) $\frac{32}{40} = \frac{4}{x}$, $x =$ _____

20) $\frac{21}{42} = \frac{x}{6}$, $x =$ _____

21) $\frac{56}{72} = \frac{7}{x}$, $x =$ _____

22) $\frac{1}{14} = \frac{x}{42}$, $x =$ _____

23) $\frac{5}{7} = \frac{75}{x}$, $x =$ _____

24) $\frac{30}{48} = \frac{x}{8}$, $x =$ _____

25) $\frac{36}{88} = \frac{9}{x}$, $x =$ _____

26) $\frac{62}{68} = \frac{x}{34}$, $x =$ _____

27) $\frac{42}{60} = \frac{x}{10}$, $x =$ _____

28) $\frac{8}{9} = \frac{x}{108}$, $x =$ _____

29) $\frac{40}{6} = \frac{x}{3}$, $x =$ _____

30) $\frac{88}{121} = \frac{x}{11}$, $x =$ _____

31) $\frac{10}{24} = \frac{x}{48}$, $x =$ _____

32) $\frac{32}{80} = \frac{x}{10}$, $x =$ _____

Chapter 4: Ratios and Proportions

Create Proportion

✎ *State if each pair of ratios form a proportion.*

1) $\frac{3}{8}$ and $\frac{24}{50}$

2) $\frac{3}{11}$ and $\frac{6}{22}$

3) $\frac{4}{5}$ and $\frac{16}{20}$

4) $\frac{5}{11}$ and $\frac{12}{33}$

5) $\frac{5}{10}$ and $\frac{15}{30}$

6) $\frac{4}{13}$ and $\frac{8}{24}$

7) $\frac{6}{9}$ and $\frac{24}{36}$

8) $\frac{7}{12}$ and $\frac{14}{20}$

9) $\frac{3}{8}$ and $\frac{27}{72}$

10) $\frac{12}{20}$ and $\frac{36}{60}$

11) $\frac{11}{12}$ and $\frac{55}{60}$

12) $\frac{12}{15}$ and $\frac{24}{25}$

13) $\frac{15}{19}$ and $\frac{20}{38}$

14) $\frac{10}{14}$ and $\frac{40}{56}$

15) $\frac{11}{13}$ and $\frac{44}{39}$

16) $\frac{15}{16}$ and $\frac{30}{32}$

17) $\frac{17}{19}$ and $\frac{34}{48}$

18) $\frac{5}{18}$ and $\frac{15}{54}$

19) $\frac{3}{14}$ and $\frac{18}{42}$

20) $\frac{7}{11}$ and $\frac{14}{32}$

21) $\frac{8}{11}$ and $\frac{32}{44}$

22) $\frac{8}{14}$ and $\frac{24}{54}$

✎ *Solve.*

23) The ratio of boys to girls in a class is 3: 4. If there are 27 boys in the class, how many girls are in that class? _____

24) The ratio of red marbles to blue marbles in a bag is 5: 6. If there are 66 marbles in the bag, how many of the marbles are red? _____

25) You can buy 6 cans of green beans at a supermarket for $3.60. How much does it cost to buy 48 cans of green beans? _____

Chapter 4: Ratios and Proportions

Similarity and Ratios

Each pair of figures is similar. Find the missing side.

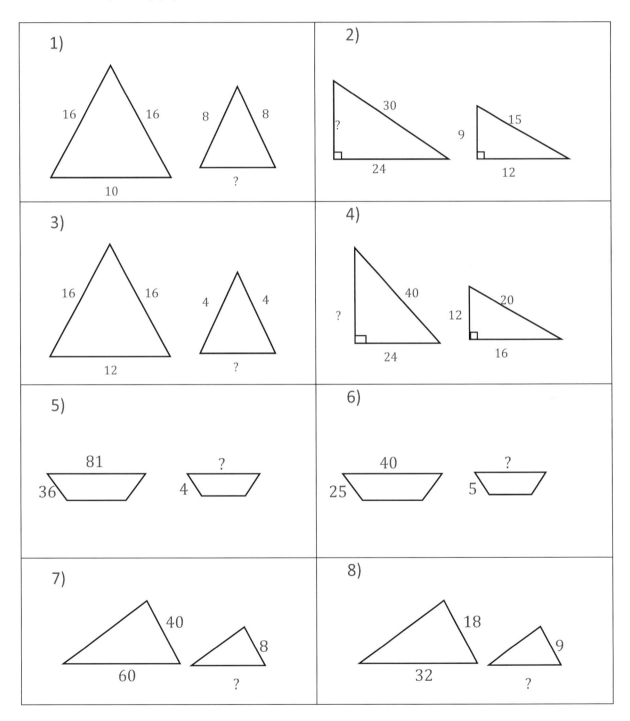

Chapter 4: Ratios and Proportions

Simple Interest

✏️ *Determine the simple interest for these loans.*

1) $400 at 6% for 4 years. $___
2) $580 at 3.5% for 5 years. $___
3) $320 at 4% for 6 years. $___
4) $510 at 8% for 3 years. $___
5) $690 at 5% for 6 months. $___
6) $620 at 7% for 3 years. $___
7) $650 at 4.5% for 10 years. $___
8) $850 at 4% for 2 years. $___
9) $640 at 7% for 3 years. $___
10) $300 at 9% for 9 months. $___
11) $760 at 8% for 2 years. $___
12) $910 at 5% for 5 years. $___
13) $540 at 3% for 6 years. $___
14) $780 at 2.5% for 4 years. $___
15) $1,600 at 7% for 3 months. $___
16) $310 at 4% for 4 years. $___
17) $950 at 6% for 5 years. $___
18) $280 at 8% for 7 years. $___
19) $310 at 6% for 3 years. $___
20) $990 at 5% for 4 months. $___

21) $380 at 6% for 5 years. $___
22) $580 at 6% for 4 years. $___
23) $1,200 at 4% for 5 years. $___
24) $3,100 at 5% for 6 years. $___
25) $5,200 at 8% for 2 years. $___
26) $1,400 at 4% for 3 years. $___
27) $300 at 3% for 8 months. $___
28) $150 at 3.5% for 4 years. $___
29) $170 at 6% for 2 years. $___
30) $940 at 8% for 5 years. $___
31) $960 at 1.5% for 8 years. $___
32) $240 at 5% for 4 months. $___
33) $280 at 2% for 5 years. $___
34) $880 at 3% for 2 years. $___
35) $2,200 at 4.5% for 2 years. $___
36) $2,400 at 7% for 3 years. $___
37) $1,800 at 5% for 6 months. $___
38) $190 at 4% for 2 years. $___
39) $480 at 6% for 5 years. $___
40) $700 at 5% for 6 years. $___

Chapter 4: Ratios and Proportions

Answers – Chapter 4

Simplifying Ratios

1) $1:7$
2) $1:4$
3) $\frac{1}{14}$
4) $\frac{2}{5}$
5) $1:3$
6) $1:6$
7) $\frac{17}{19}$
8) $\frac{5}{7}$
9) $2:9$
10) $2:3$
11) $\frac{5}{8}$
12) $\frac{1}{11}$
13) $2:3$
14) $4:5$
15) $\frac{1}{2}$
16) $\frac{3}{11}$
17) $1:3$
18) 1 to 4
19) $\frac{8}{9}$
20) $\frac{3}{4}$
21) $4:5$
22) $1:3$
23) $\frac{2}{3}$
24) $\frac{6}{13}$
25) $1:4$
26) $1:4$
27) $\frac{1}{5}$
28) $\frac{23}{26}$

Proportional Ratios

1) $x = 14$
2) $x = 6$
3) $x = 20$
4) $x = 15$
5) $x = 55$
6) $x = 18$
7) $x = 38$
8) $x = 14$
9) $x = 63$
10) $x = 45$
11) $x = 104$
12) $x = 48$
13) $x = 57$
14) $x = 30$
15) $x = 5$
16) $x = 54$
17) $x = 81$
18) $x = 6$
19) $x = 5$
20) $x = 3$
21) $x = 9$
22) $x = 3$
23) $x = 105$
24) $x = 5$
25) $x = 22$
26) $x = 31$
27) $x = 7$
28) $x = 96$
29) $x = 20$
30) $x = 8$
31) $x = 20$
32) $x = 4$

Chapter 4: Ratios and Proportions

Create Proportion

1) No
2) Yes
3) Yes
4) No
5) Yes
6) No
7) Yes
8) No
9) Yes
10) Yes
11) Yes
12) No
13) No
14) Yes
15) No
16) Yes
17) No
18) Yes
19) No
20) No
21) Yes
22) No
23) 36 girls
24) 30 red marbles
25) $28.80

Similarity and Ratios

1) 5
2) 18
3) 3
4) 32
5) 9
6) 8
7) 12
8) 16

Chapter 4: Ratios and Proportions

Simple Interest

1) $96
2) $101.50
3) $76.80
4) $122.40
5) $17.25
6) $130.20
7) $292.50
8) $68
9) $134.40
10) $20.25
11) $121.60
12) $227.50
13) $97.20
14) $78
15) $28
16) $49.60
17) $285
18) $156.80
19) $55.80
20) $16.5
21) $114
22) $139.20
23) $240
24) $930
25) $832
26) $168
27) $6
28) $21
29) $20.40
30) $376
31) $115.20
32) $4
33) $28
34) $52.80
35) $198
36) $504
37) $45
38) $15.20
39) $144
40) $210

Chapter 5: Percentage

Math Topics that you'll learn in this Chapter:

- ✓ Percent Problems
- ✓ Percent of Increase and Decrease
- ✓ Discount, Tax and Tip

Chapter 5: Percentage

Percent Problems

Solve each problem.

1) What is 4 percent of 280? ____
2) What is 25 percent of 500? ____
3) What is 10 percent of 460? ____
4) What is 34 percent of 260? ____
5) What is 60 percent of 850? ____
6) 63 is what percent of 300? ____%
7) 80 is what percent of 400? ____%
8) 70 is what percent of 700? ____%
9) 84 is what percent of 600? ____%
10) 90 is what percent of 300? ____%
11) 24 is what percent of 150? ____%
12) 12 is what percent of 80? ____%
13) 4 is what percent of 50? ____%
14) 110 is what percent of 500? ____%
15) 16 is what percent of 400? ____%

16) 39 is what percent of 300? ____%
17) 56 is what percent of 200? ____%
18) 30 is what percent of 500? ____%
19) 84 is what percent of 700? ____%
20) 40 is what percent of 500? ____%
21) 26 is what percent of 100? ____%
22) 45 is what percent of 900? ____%
23) 60 is what percent of 400? ____%
24) 18 is what percent of 900? ____%
25) 75 is what percent of 250? ____%
26) 27 is what percent of 900? ____%
27) 49 is what percent of 700? ____%
28) 81 is what percent of 900? ____%
29) 90 is what percent of 500? ____%
30) 82 is what percent of 410? ____%

31) 14 is 35 percent of what number? ____
32) 90 is 6 percent of what number? ____
33) 80 is 40 percent of what number? ____
34) 80 is 20 percent of what number? ____
35) 30 is 6 percent of what number? ____
36) 64 is 8 percent of what number? ____

Chapter 5: Percentage

Percent of Increase and Decrease

✍ *Solve each percent of change word problem.*

1) Bob got a raise, and his hourly wage increased from $30 to $42. What is the percent increase? _____ %

2) The price of gasoline rose from $4.40 to $4.62 in one month. By what percent did the gas price rise? _____ %

3) In a class, the number of students has been increased from 25 to 32. What is the percent increase? _____ %

4) The price of a pair of shoes increases from $24 to $30. What is the percent increase? ___ %

5) In a class, the number of students has been decreased from 24 to 18. What is the percentage decrease? _____ %

6) Nick got a raise, and his hourly wage increased from $50 to $55. What is the percent increase? _____ %

7) A coat was originally priced at $60. It went on sale for $54. What was the percent that the coat was discounted? _____ %

8) The price of a pair of shoes increases from $12 to $18. What is the percent increase? ___ %

9) A house was purchased in 2002 for $150,000. It is now valued at $132,000. What is the rate (percent) of depreciation for the house? ____ %

10) The price of gasoline rose from $4.00 to $4.20 in one month. By what percent did the gas price rise? _____ %

Chapter 5: Percentage

Discount, Tax and Tip

✎ *Find the missing values.*

1) Original price of a computer: $540, Tax: 6%, Selling price: $_____

2) Original price of a sofa: $400, Tax: 14%, Selling price: $_____

3) Original price of a table: $560, Tax: 15%, Selling price: $_____

4) Original price of a cell phone: $740, Tax: 24%, Selling price: $_____

5) Original price of a printer: $400, Tax: 22%, Selling price: $_____

6) Original price of a computer: $600, Tax: 15%, Selling price: $_____

7) Restaurant bill: $24.00, Tip: 25%, Final amount: $_____

8) Original price of a cell phone: $300 Tax: 8%, Selling price: $_____

9) Original price of a carpet: $800, Tax: 25%, Selling price: $_____

10) Original price of a camera: $200 Discount: 35%, Selling price: $_____

11) Original price of a dress: $560 Discount: 10%, Selling price: $_____

12) Original price of a monitor: $420 Discount: 6%, Selling price: $_____

13) Original price of a laptop: $880 Discount: 16%, Selling price: $_____

14) Restaurant bill: $64.00, Tip: 20%, Final amount: $_____

Chapter 5: Percentage

Answers – Chapter 5

Percent Problems

1) 11.2
2) 125
3) 46
4) 88.4
5) 510
6) 21%
7) 20%
8) 10%
9) 14%
10) 30%
11) 16%
12) 15%
13) 8%
14) 22%
15) 4%
16) 13%
17) 28%
18) 6%
19) 12%
20) 8%
21) 26%
22) 5%
23) 15%
24) 2%
25) 30%
26) 3%
27) 7%
28) 9%
29) 18%
30) 20%
31) 40
32) 1,500
33) 200
34) 400
35) 500
36) 800

Percent of Increase and Decrease

1) 40%
2) 5%
3) 28%
4) 25%
5) 25%
6) 10%
7) 10%
8) 50%
9) 12%
10) 5%

Chapter 5: Percentage

Discount, Tax and Tip

1) $572.40
2) $456
3) $644
4) $917.60
5) $488
6) $690
7) $30.00
8) $324
9) $1,000
10) $130
11) $504
12) $394.8
13) $739.2
14) $76.80

Chapter 6: Expressions and Variables

Math Topics that you'll learn in this Chapter:

- ✓ Simplifying Variable Expressions
- ✓ Simplifying Polynomial Expressions
- ✓ Evaluating One Variable
- ✓ Evaluating Two Variables
- ✓ The Distributive Property

Chapter 6: Expressions and Variables

Simplifying Variable Expressions

✏️ *Simplify and write the answer.*

1) $6x + 2 + 3x =$

2) $7x + 4 - 6x =$

3) $-1 - x^2 - 9x^2 =$

4) $(-5)(6x - 2) =$

5) $3 + 10x^2 + 2x =$

6) $8x^2 + 6x + 7x^2 =$

7) $2x^2 - 5x - 7x =$

8) $x - 3 + 5 - 3x =$

9) $2 - 3x + 12 - 2x =$

10) $5x^2 - 12x^2 + 8x =$

11) $2x^2 + 6x + 3x^2 =$

12) $2x^2 - 2x - x =$

13) $2x^2 - (-8x + 6) =$

14) $4x + 6(2 - 5x) =$

15) $10x + 8(10x - 6) =$

16) $9(-2x - 6) - 5 =$

17) $32x - 4 + 23 + 2x =$

18) $8x - 12x - x^2 + 13 =$

19) $(-6)(8x - 4) + 10x =$

20) $14x - 5(5 - 8x) =$

21) $23x + 4(9x + 3) + 12 =$

22) $3(-7x + 5) + 20x =$

23) $12x - 3x(x + 9) =$

24) $7x + 5x(3 - 3x) =$

25) $5x(-8x + 12) + 14x =$

26) $40x + 12 + 2x^2 =$

27) $5x(x - 3) - 10 =$

28) $8x - 7 + 8x + 2x^2 =$

29) $6x - 2x^2 - 6x^2 - 5 =$

30) $3 + x^2 - 4x^2 - 10x =$

31) $10x + 6x^2 + 5x + 18 =$

32) $20 + 12x^2 + 7x - 6x^2 =$

Chapter 6: Expressions and Variables

Simplifying Polynomial Expressions

✍ *Simplify and write the answer.*

1) $(3x^3 + 4x^2) - (10x + 3x^2) =$ _____

2) $(-4x^5 + 4x^3) - (6x^3 + 5x^2) =$ _____

3) $(10x^4 + 6x^2) - (x^2 - 8x^4) =$ _____

4) $6x - 2x^2 - 3(2x^2 + 5x^3) =$ _____

5) $(2x^3 - 3) + 3(2x^2 - 3x^3) =$ _____

6) $4(4x^3 - 2x) - (3x^3 - 2x^4) =$ _____

7) $2(4x - 3x^3) - 3(3x^3 + 4x^2) =$ _____

8) $(2x^2 - 2x) - (2x^3 + 5x^2) =$ _____

9) $2x^3 - (4x^4 + 2x) + x^2 =$ _____

10) $x^4 - 9(x^2 + x) - 5x =$ _____

11) $(-2x^2 - x^4) + (4x^4 - x^2) =$ _____

12) $4x^2 - 5x^3 + 15x^4 - 12x^3 =$ _____

13) $3x^2 - 2x^4 + 12x^4 - 10x^3 =$ _____

14) $4x^2 + 6x^3 - 8x^2 + 14x =$ _____

15) $3x^4 - 6x^5 + 7x^4 - 9x^2 =$ _____

16) $5x^3 + 15x - 4x^2 - 3x^3 =$ _____

Chapter 6: Expressions and Variables

Evaluating One Variable

✏️ *Evaluate each expression using the value given.*

1) $x = 2 \Rightarrow 5x - 10 =$

2) $x = 3 \Rightarrow 6x - 12 =$

3) $x = 4 \Rightarrow 6x + 8 =$

4) $x = 6 \Rightarrow 2x + 4 =$

5) $x = 4 \Rightarrow 4x - 8 =$

6) $x = 2 \Rightarrow 5x - 2x + 10 =$

7) $x = 3 \Rightarrow 2x - x - 6 =$

8) $x = 4 \Rightarrow 6x - 3x + 4 =$

9) $x = -2 \Rightarrow 4x - 6x - 5 =$

10) $x = -1 \Rightarrow 3x - 5x + 11 =$

11) $x = 1 \Rightarrow x - 7x + 12 =$

12) $x = 2 \Rightarrow 2(-3x + 4) =$

13) $x = 3 \Rightarrow 4(-5x - 2) =$

14) $x = 2 \Rightarrow 5(-2x - 4) =$

15) $x = -2 \Rightarrow 3(-4x - 5) =$

16) $x = 3 \Rightarrow 8x + 5 =$

17) $x = -3 \Rightarrow 12x + 9 =$

18) $x = -1 \Rightarrow 9x - 8 =$

19) $x = 2 \Rightarrow 16x - 10 =$

20) $x = 1 \Rightarrow 4x + 3 =$

21) $x = 5 \Rightarrow 7x - 2 =$

22) $x = 7 \Rightarrow 28 - x =$

23) $x = 8 \Rightarrow 4x - 12 =$

24) $x = 10 \Rightarrow 44 - 3x =$

25) $x = 4 \Rightarrow 10x - 6 =$

26) $x = 7 \Rightarrow 6x - x + 9 =$

Chapter 6: Expressions and Variables

Evaluating Two Variables

✏️ *Evaluate each expression using the values given.*

1) $x + 4y, x = 3, y = 2$ _____

2) $6x + 3y, x = -2, y = -3$ _____

3) $x + 5y, x = 2, y = -1$ _____

4) $3a - (10 - b), a = 3, b = 4$ _____

5) $4a - (6 - 3b), a = 1, b = 4$ _____

6) $a - (8 - 2b), a = 2, b = 5$ _____

7) $3z + 21 + 5k, z = 4, k = 1$ _____

8) $-7a + 4b, a = 6, b = 3$ _____

9) $-4a + 3b, a = 2, b = 4$ _____

10) $-6a + 6b, a = 4, b = 3$ _____

11) $-8a + 2b, a = 4, b = 6$ _____

12) $4x + 6y, x = 6, y = 3$ _____

13) $2x + 9y, x = 8, y = 1$ _____

14) $x - 7y, x = 9, y = 4$ _____

15) $5x - 4y, x = 6, y = 3$ _____

16) $2z + 14 + 8k, z = 4, k = 1$ _____

17) $6x + 3y, x = 3, y = 8$ _____

18) $5a - 6b, a = -3, b = -1$ _____

19) $6a + 2b, a = -6, b = 4$ _____

20) $-3a - b, a = 5, b = -6$ _____

21) $-6a + 2b, a = 6, b = -3$ _____

22) $-6a + 8b, a = 6, b = -1$ _____

Chapter 6: Expressions and Variables

The Distributive Property

✏️ *Use the distributive property to simply each expression.*

1) $(-2)(10x + 3) =$

2) $(-3x + 5)(-5) =$

3) $11(-3x + 3) =$

4) $6(5 - 4x) =$

5) $(6 - 5x)(-4) =$

6) $9(8 - 2x) =$

7) $(-4x + 6)5 =$

8) $(-2x + 7)(-8) =$

9) $8(-4x + 7) =$

10) $(-9x + 5)(-3) =$

11) $8(-x + 9) =$

12) $7(2 - 6x) =$

13) $(-12x + 4)(-3) =$

14) $(-6)(-10x + 6) =$

15) $(-5)(5 - 11x) =$

16) $9(4 - 8x) =$

17) $(-6x + 2)7 =$

18) $(-9)(1 - 12x) =$

19) $(-3)(4 - 6x) =$

20) $(2 - 8x)(-2) =$

21) $20(2 - x) =$

22) $12(-4x + 3) =$

23) $12(3 - 4x) =$

24) $(-6x + 6)3 =$

25) $(-10x + 6)(-3) =$

26) $13(4 - 7x) =$

Chapter 6: Expressions and Variables

Answers – Chapter 6

Simplifying Variable Expressions

1) $9x + 2$

2) $x + 4$

3) $-10x^2 - 1$

4) $-30x + 10$

5) $10x^2 + 2x + 3$

6) $15x^2 + 6x$

7) $2x^2 - 12x$

8) $-2x + 2$

9) $-5x + 14$

10) $-7x^2 + 8x$

11) $5x^2 + 6x$

12) $2x^2 - 3x$

13) $2x^2 + 8x - 6$

14) $-26x + 12$

15) $90x - 48$

16) $-18x - 59$

17) $34x + 19$

18) $-x^2 - 4x + 13$

19) $-38x + 24$

20) $54x - 25$

21) $59x + 24$

22) $-x + 15$

23) $-3x^2 - 15x$

24) $-15x^2 + 22x$

25) $-40x^2 + 74x$

26) $2x^2 + 40x + 12$

27) $5x^2 - 15x - 10$

28) $2x^2 + 16x - 7$

29) $-8x^2 + 6x - 5$

30) $-3x^2 - 10x + 3$

31) $6x^2 + 15x + 18$

32) $6x^2 + 7x + 20$

Chapter 6: Expressions and Variables

Simplifying Polynomial Expressions

1) $3x^3 + x^2 - 10x$

2) $-4x^5 - 2x^3 - 5x^2$

3) $18x^4 + 5x^2$

4) $-15x^3 - 8x^2 + 6x$

5) $-7x^3 + 6x^2 - 3$

6) $2x^4 + 13x^3 - 8x$

7) $-15x^3 - 12x^2 + 8x$

8) $-2x^3 - 3x^2 - 2x$

9) $-4x^4 + 2x^3 + x^2 - 2x$

10) $x^4 - 9x^2 - 14x$

11) $3x^4 - 3x^2$

12) $15x^4 - 17x^3 + 4x^2$

13) $10x^4 - 10x^3 + 3x^2$

14) $6x^3 - 4x^2 + 14x$

15) $-6x^5 + 10x^4 - 9x^2$

16) $2x^3 - 4x^2 + 15x$

Evaluating One Variable

1) 0
2) 6
3) 32
4) 16
5) 8
6) 16
7) −3

8) 16
9) −1
10) 13
11) 6
12) −4
13) −68
14) −40

15) 9
16) 29
17) −27
18) −17
19) 22
20) 7
21) 33

22) 21
23) 20
24) 14
25) 34
26) 44

Chapter 6: Expressions and Variables

Evaluating Two Variables

1) 11
2) −21
3) −3
4) 3
5) 10
6) 4
7) 38
8) −30
9) 4
10) −6
11) −20
12) 42
13) 25
14) −19
15) 18
16) 30
17) 42
18) −9
19) −28
20) −9
21) −42
22) −44

The Distributive Property

1) $-20x - 6$
2) $15x - 25$
3) $-33x + 33$
4) $-24x + 30$
5) $20x - 24$
6) $-18x + 72$
7) $-20x + 30$
8) $16x - 56$
9) $-32x + 56$
10) $27x - 15$
11) $-8x + 72$
12) $-42x + 14$
13) $36x - 12$
14) $60x - 36$
15) $55x - 25$
16) $-72x + 36$
17) $-42x + 14$
18) $108x - 9$
19) $18x - 12$
20) $16x - 4$
21) $-20x + 40$
22) $-48x + 36$
23) $-48x + 36$
24) $-18x + 18$
25) $30x - 18$
26) $-91x + 52$

Chapter 7: Equations and Inequalities

Math Topics that you'll learn in this Chapter:

- ✓ One–Step Equations
- ✓ Multi–Step Equations
- ✓ System of Equations
- ✓ Graphing Single–Variable Inequalities
- ✓ One–Step Inequalities
- ✓ Multi–Step Inequalities

Chapter 7: Equations and Inequalities

One–Step Equations

✏️ *Solve each equation for x.*

1) $x - 18 = 28 \Rightarrow x = $ _____

2) $19 = -5 + x \Rightarrow x = $ _____

3) $15 - x = 6 \Rightarrow x = $ _____

4) $x - 24 = 29 \Rightarrow x = $ _____

5) $24 - x = 17 \Rightarrow x = $ _____

6) $16 - x = 3 \Rightarrow x = $ _____

7) $x + 14 = 12 \Rightarrow x = $ _____

8) $26 + x = 8 \Rightarrow x = $ _____

9) $x + 9 = -18 \Rightarrow x = $ _____

10) $x + 21 = 11 \Rightarrow x = $ _____

11) $17 = -5 + x \Rightarrow x = $ _____

12) $x + 20 = 29 \Rightarrow x = $ _____

13) $x - 13 = 19 \Rightarrow x = $ _____

14) $x + 9 = -17 \Rightarrow x = $ _____

15) $x + 4 = -23 \Rightarrow x = $ _____

16) $16 = -9 + x \Rightarrow x = $ _____

17) $4x = 28 \Rightarrow x = $ _____

18) $21 = -7x \Rightarrow x = $ _____

19) $12x = -12 \Rightarrow x = $ _____

20) $13x = 39 \Rightarrow x = $ _____

21) $8x = -16 \Rightarrow x = $ _____

22) $\frac{x}{2} = -5 \Rightarrow x = $ _____

23) $\frac{x}{9} = 6 \Rightarrow x = $ _____

24) $27 = \frac{x}{5} \Rightarrow x = $ _____

25) $\frac{x}{4} = -3 \Rightarrow x = $ _____

26) $x \div 8 = 7 \Rightarrow x = $ _____

27) $x \div 2 = -3 \Rightarrow x = $ _____

28) $8x = 56 \Rightarrow x = $ _____

29) $9x = 54 \Rightarrow x = $ _____

30) $7x = -35 \Rightarrow x = $ _____

31) $60 = -10x \Rightarrow x = $ _____

Chapter 7: Equations and Inequalities

Multi –Step Equations

✍ **Solve each equation.**

1) $4x - 7 = 13 \Rightarrow x =$ ____

2) $26 = -(x - 4) \Rightarrow x =$ ____

3) $-(5 - x) = 19 \Rightarrow x =$ ____

4) $35 = -x + 14 \Rightarrow x =$ ____

5) $2(3 - 2x) = 10 \Rightarrow x =$ ____

6) $3x - 3 = 15 \Rightarrow x =$ ____

7) $32 = -x + 15 \Rightarrow x =$ ____

8) $-(10 - x) = -13 \Rightarrow x =$ ____

9) $-4(7 + x) = 4 \Rightarrow x =$ ____

10) $22 = 2x - 8 \Rightarrow x =$ ____

11) $-6(3 + x) = 6 \Rightarrow x =$ ____

12) $-3 = 3x - 15 \Rightarrow x =$ ____

13) $-7(12 + x) = 7 \Rightarrow x =$ ____

14) $8(6 - 4x) = 16 \Rightarrow x =$ ____

15) $18 - 4x = -9 - x \Rightarrow x =$ ____

16) $6(4 - x) = 30 \Rightarrow x =$ ____

17) $15 - 3x = -5 - x \Rightarrow x =$ ____

18) $9(-7 - 3x) = 18 \Rightarrow x =$ ____

19) $16 - 2x = -4 - 7x \Rightarrow x =$ ____

20) $14 - 2x = 14 + x \Rightarrow x =$ ____

21) $21 - 3x = -7 - 10x \Rightarrow x =$ ____

22) $8 - 2x = 11 + x \Rightarrow x =$ ____

23) $10 + 12x = -8 + 6x \Rightarrow x =$ ____

24) $25 + 20x = -5 + 5x \Rightarrow x =$ ____

25) $16 - x = -8 - 7x \Rightarrow x =$ ____

26) $17 - 3x = 13 + x \Rightarrow x =$ ____

27) $22 + 5x = -8 - x \Rightarrow x =$ ____

28) $-9(7 + x) = 9 \Rightarrow x =$ ____

29) $12 + 2x = -4 - 2x \Rightarrow x =$ ____

30) $12 - x = 2 - 3x \Rightarrow x =$ ____

31) $19 - x = -1 - 11x \Rightarrow x =$ ____

32) $14 - 3x = -5 - 4x \Rightarrow x =$ ____

Chapter 7: Equations and Inequalities

System of Equations

✎ *Solve each system of equations.*

1) $2x + 3y = 15$ $x =$
   $x - 3y = 3$ $y =$

2) $y = x + 3$ $x =$
   $x + y = -5$ $y =$

3) $x + 3y = 6$ $x =$
   $2x + 8y = -12$ $y =$

4) $2x + y = 5$ $x =$
   $-3x + 6y = 0$ $y =$

5) $10x - 8y = -15$ $x =$
   $-6x + 4y = 13$ $y =$

6) $-3x - 4y = 5$ $x =$
   $x - 2y = 5$ $y =$

7) $5x - 12y = -19$ $x =$
   $-6x + 7y = 8$ $y =$

8) $5x - 7y = -2$ $x =$
   $-x - 2y = -3$ $y =$

9) $-x + 3y = 3$ $x =$
   $-7x + 8y = -5$ $y =$

10) $-4x + 3y = -18$ $x =$
    $4x - y = 14$ $y =$

11) $6x - 7y = -8$ $x =$
    $-x - 4y = -9$ $y =$

12) $-3x + 2y = -16$ $x =$
    $4x - y = 13$ $y =$

13) $2x + 3y = 8$ $x =$
    $-3x + 2y = 1$ $y =$

14) $y = -x + 3$ $x =$
    $3y + 5x = -1$ $y =$

15) $2x + 3y = 12$ $x =$
    $x + y = 5$ $y =$

16) $y = x - 1$ $x =$
    $y = 2x + 2$ $y =$

Chapter 7: Equations and Inequalities

Graphing Single–Variable Inequalities

✎ **Graph each inequality.**

1) $x < 5$

2) $x \geq 2$
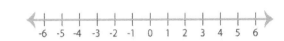

3) $x \geq -4$

4) $x \leq -1$

5) $x > -1$

6) $3 > x$

7) $2 \leq x$

8) $x > 0$

9) $-3 \leq x$

10) $-4 \leq x$

11) $x \leq 6$

12) $1 \leq x$

13) $-4 < x$

14) $x > -5$

Chapter 7: Equations and Inequalities

One–Step Inequalities

✏️ *Solve each inequality for x.*

1) $x - 9 < 20 \Rightarrow$ _____

2) $14 \leq -6 + x \Rightarrow$ _____

3) $x - 31 > 9 \Rightarrow$ _____

4) $x + 28 \geq 36 \Rightarrow$ _____

5) $x - 24 > 17 \Rightarrow$ _____

6) $x + 5 \geq 3 \Rightarrow x$ _____

7) $x + 14 < 12 \Rightarrow$ _____

8) $26 + x \leq 8 \Rightarrow$ _____

9) $x + 9 \geq -18 \Rightarrow$ _____

10) $x + 24 < 11 \Rightarrow$ _____

11) $17 \leq -5 + x \Rightarrow$ _____

12) $x + 25 > 29 \Rightarrow x$ _____

13) $x - 17 \geq 19 \Rightarrow$ _____

14) $x + 8 > -17 \Rightarrow$ _____

15) $x + 8 < -23 \Rightarrow$ _____

16) $16 \leq -5 + x \Rightarrow$ _____

17) $4x \leq 12 \Rightarrow$ _____

18) $28 \geq -7x \Rightarrow$ _____

19) $2x > -14 \Rightarrow$ _____

20) $13x \leq 39 \Rightarrow$ _____

21) $-8x > -16 \Rightarrow$ _____

22) $\frac{x}{2} < -6 \Rightarrow$ _____

23) $\frac{x}{6} > 6 \Rightarrow$ _____

24) $27 \leq \frac{x}{4} \Rightarrow$ _____

25) $\frac{x}{8} < -3 \Rightarrow$ _____

26) $6x \geq 18 \Rightarrow$ _____

27) $5x \geq -25 \Rightarrow$ _____

28) $3x > 45 \Rightarrow$ _____

29) $9x \leq 72 \Rightarrow$ _____

30) $-6x < -36 \Rightarrow$ _____

31) $70 > -10x \Rightarrow$ _____

Chapter 7: Equations and Inequalities

Multi –Step Inequalities

Solve each inequality.

1) $2x - 6 \leq 4 \rightarrow$ _____

2) $2 + 3x \geq 17 \rightarrow$ _____

3) $9 + 3x \geq 36 \rightarrow$ _____

4) $2x - 6 \leq 18 \rightarrow$ _____

5) $3x - 4 \leq 23 \rightarrow$ _____

6) $7x - 5 \leq 51 \rightarrow$ _____

7) $4x - 9 \leq 27 \rightarrow$ _____

8) $6x - 11 \leq 13 \rightarrow$ _____

9) $5x - 7 \leq 33 \rightarrow$ _____

10) $6 + 2x \geq 28 \rightarrow$ _____

11) $8 + 3x \geq 35 \rightarrow$ _____

12) $4 + 6x < 34 \rightarrow$ _____

13) $3 + 2x \geq 53 \rightarrow$ _____

14) $7 - 6x > 56 + x \rightarrow$ _____

15) $9 + 4x \geq 39 + 2x \rightarrow$ _____

16) $3 + 5x \geq 43 \rightarrow$ _____

17) $4 - 7x < 60 \rightarrow$ _____

18) $11 - 4x \geq 55 \rightarrow$ _____

19) $12 + x \geq 48 - 2x \rightarrow$ _____

20) $10 - 10x \leq -20 \rightarrow$ _____

21) $5 - 9x \geq -40 \rightarrow$ _____

22) $8 - 7x \geq 36 \rightarrow$ _____

23) $6 + 10x < 69 + 3x \rightarrow$ _____

24) $5 + 4x < 26 - 3x \rightarrow$ _____

25) $10 + 11x < 59 + 4x \rightarrow$ _____

26) $3 + 9x \geq 48 - 6x \rightarrow$ _____

Chapter 7: Equations and Inequalities

Answers – Chapter 7

One–Step Equations

1) $x = 46$
2) $x = 24$
3) $x = 9$
4) $x = 53$
5) $x = 7$
6) $x = 13$
7) $x = -2$
8) $x = -18$
9) $x = -27$
10) $x = -10$
11) $x = 22$
12) $x = 9$
13) $x = 32$
14) $x = -26$
15) $x = -27$
16) $x = 25$
17) $x = 7$
18) $x = -3$
19) $x = -1$
20) $x = 3$
21) $x = -2$
22) $x = -10$
23) $x = 54$
24) $x = 135$
25) $x = -12$
26) $x = 56$
27) $x = -6$
28) $x = 7$
29) $x = 6$
30) $x = -5$
31) $x = -6$

Multi–Step Equations

1) $x = 5$
2) $x = -22$
3) $x = 24$
4) $x = -21$
5) $x = -1$
6) $x = 6$
7) $x = -17$
8) $x = -3$
9) $x = -8$
10) $x = 15$
11) $x = -4$
12) $x = 4$
13) $x = -13$
14) $x = 1$
15) $x = 9$
16) $x = -1$
17) $x = 10$
18) $x = -3$
19) $x = -4$
20) $x = 0$
21) $x = -4$
22) $x = -1$
23) $x = -3$
24) $x = -2$
25) $x = -4$
26) $x = 1$
27) $x = -5$
28) $x = -8$
29) $x = -4$
30) $x = -5$
31) $x = -2$
32) $x = -19$

Chapter 7: Equations and Inequalities

System of Equations

1) $x = 6, y = 1$

2) $x = -4, y = -1$

3) $x = 42, y = -12$

4) $x = 2, y = 1$

5) $x = -\frac{11}{2}, y = -5$

6) $x = 1, y = -2$

7) $x = 1, y = 2$

8) $x = 1, y = 1$

9) $x = 3, y = 2$

10) $x = 3, y = -2$

11) $x = 1, y = 2$

12) $x = 2, y = -5$

13) $x = 1, y = 2$

14) $x = -5, y = 8$

15) $x = 3, y = 2$

16) $x = -3, y = -4$

Chapter 7: Equations and Inequalities

Graphing Single–Variable Inequalities

1) $x < 5$

2) $x \geq 2$

3) $x \geq -4$

4) $x \leq -1$

5) $x > -1$

6) $3 > x$

7) $2 \leq x$

8) $x > 0$

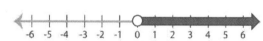

9) $-3 \leq x$

10) $-4 \leq x$

11) $x \leq 6$

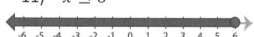

12) $1 \leq x$

13) $-4 < x$

14) $x > -5$

Chapter 7: Equations and Inequalities

One–Step Inequalities

1) $x < 29$
2) $20 \leq x$
3) $x > 40$
4) $x \geq 8$
5) $x > 41$
6) $x \geq -2$
7) $x < -2$
8) $x \leq -18$
9) $x \geq -27$
10) $x < -13$
11) $22 \leq x$
12) $x > 4$
13) $x \geq 36$
14) $x > -25$
15) $x < -31$
16) $21 \leq x$
17) $x \leq 3$
18) $-4 \leq x$
19) $x > -7$
20) $x \leq 3$
21) $x < 2$
22) $x < -12$
23) $x > 36$
24) $108 \leq x$
25) $x < -24$
26) $x \geq 3$
27) $x \geq -5$
28) $x > 15$
29) $x \leq 8$
30) $x > 6$
31) $-7 < x$

Multi–Step Inequalities

1) $x \leq 5$
2) $x \geq 5$
3) $x \geq 9$
4) $x \leq 12$
5) $x \leq 9$
6) $x \leq 8$
7) $x \leq 9$
8) $x \leq 4$
9) $x \leq 8$
10) $x \geq 11$
11) $x \geq 9$
12) $x < 5$
13) $x \geq 25$
14) $x < -7$
15) $x \geq 15$
16) $x \geq 8$
17) $x > -8$
18) $x \leq -11$
19) $x \geq 12$
20) $x \geq 3$
21) $x \leq 5$
22) $x \leq -4$
23) $x < 9$
24) $x < 3$
25) $x < 7$
26) $x \geq 3$

Chapter 8: Lines and Slope

Math Topics that you'll learn in this Chapter:

- ✓ Finding Slope
- ✓ Graphing Lines Using Slope–Intercept Form
- ✓ Writing Linear Equations
- ✓ Graphing Linear Inequalities
- ✓ Finding Midpoint
- ✓ Finding Distance of Two Points

Chapter 8: Lines and Slope

Finding Slope

✎ *Find the slope of each line.*

1) $y = 2x - 8$, Slope =

2) $y = -6x + 3$, Slope =

3) $y = -x - 5$, Slope =

4) $y = -2x - 9$, Slope =

5) $y = 5 + 2x$, Slope =

6) $y = 1 - 8x$, Slope =

7) $y = -4x + 3$, Slope =

8) $y = -9x + 8$, Slope =

9) $y = -2x + 4$, Slope =

10) $y = 9x - 8$, Slope =

11) $y = \frac{1}{2}x + 4$, Slope =

12) $y = -\frac{2}{5}x + 7$, Slope =

13) $-x + 3y = 5$, Slope =

14) $4x + 4y = 6$, Slope =

15) $6y - 2x = 10$, Slope =

16) $3y - x = 2$, Slope =

✎ *Find the slope of the line through each pair of points.*

17) $(4, 4), (8, 12)$, Slope =

23) $(8, 4), (9, 6)$, Slope =

18) $(-2, 4), (0, 6)$, Slope =

24) $(10, -1), (7, 8)$, Slope =

19) $(6, -2), (2, 6)$, Slope =

25) $(16, -3), (13, -6)$, Slope =

20) $(-4, -2), (0, 6)$, Slope =

26) $(12, 5), (8, 1)$, Slope =

21) $(6, 2), (3, 5)$, Slope =

27) $(6, 6), (8, 10)$, Slope =

22) $(-5, 1), (-1, 9)$, Slope =

28) $(10, -1), (8, 1)$, Slope =

Chapter 8: Lines and Slope

Graphing Lines Using Slope–Intercept Form

Sketch the graph of each line.

1) $y = -x + 1$

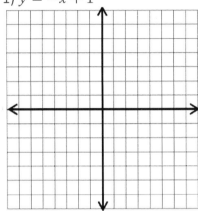

2) $y = 2x - 4$

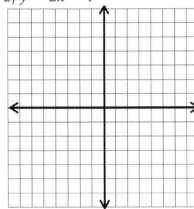

3) $y = -x + 6$

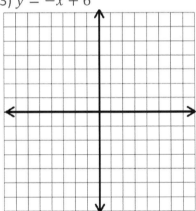

4) $y = x - 4$

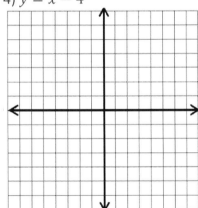

5) $y = 2x - 2$

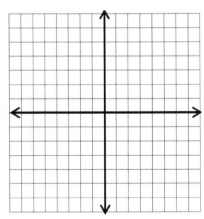

6) $y = -\frac{1}{2}x + 2$

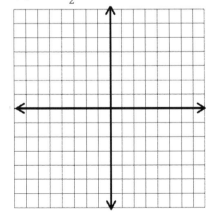

Chapter 8: Lines and Slope

Writing Linear Equations

✎ *Write the equation of the line through the given points.*

1) through: $(2, -2), (3, 4)$ $y =$

2) through: $(-2, 4), (1, 7)$ $y =$

3) through: $(-1, 3), (3, 7)$ $y =$

4) through: $(6, 5), (3, 2)$ $y =$

5) through: $(7, -10), (2, 10)$ $y =$

6) through: $(7, 2), (6, 1)$ $y =$

7) through: $(6, -1), (4, 1)$ $y =$

8) through: $(-2, 8), (-4, -6)$ $y =$

9) through: $(-2, 5), (-3, 4)$ $y =$

10) through: $(6, 8), (8, -6)$ $y =$

11) through: $(-2, 5), (-4, -3)$ $y =$

12) through: $(8, 8), (4, -8)$ $y =$

13) through: $(7, -4)$, Slope: -1 $y =$

14) through: $(4, -10)$, Slope: -2 $y =$

15) through: $(6, 10)$, Slope: 9 $y =$

16) through: $(-6, 8)$, Slope: -2 $y =$

✎ *Solve each problem.*

17) What is the equation of a line with slope 6 and intercept 4? _____

18) What is the equation of a line with slope 5 and intercept 9? _____

19) What is the equation of a line with slope 8 and passes through point $(2, 8)$?
_____

20) What is the equation of a line with slope -3 and passes through point $(-4, 10)$? _____

Chapter 8: Lines and Slope

Finding Midpoint

Find the midpoint of the line segment with the given endpoints.

1) $(4, 4), (0, 4)$, midpoint = (__, __)

2) $(5, 1), (-1, 5)$, midpoint = (__, __)

3) $(4, -2), (0, 6)$, midpoint = (__, __)

4) $(-3, 3), (-1, 5)$, midpoint = (__, __)

5) $(5, -2), (9, -6)$, midpoint = (__, __)

6) $(-6, -3), (4, -7)$, midpoint = (__, __)

7) $(7, 0), (-7, 8)$, midpoint = (__, __)

8) $(-8, 4), (-4, 0)$, midpoint = (__, __)

9) $(-3, 6), (9, -8)$, midpoint = (__, __)

10) $(6, 8), (6, -6)$, midpoint = (__, __)

11) $(6, 7), (-8, 5)$, midpoint = (__, __)

12) $(9, 3), (-3, -9)$, midpoint = (__, __)

13) $(-6, 12), (-4, 6)$, midpoint = (__, __)

14) $(10, 7), (8, -3)$, midpoint = (__, __)

15) $(13, 7), (-5, 3)$, midpoint = (__, __)

16) $(-9, -4), (-5, 8)$, midpoint = (__, __)

17) $(12, 5), (6, 15)$, midpoint = (__, __)

18) $(-6, -10), (12, -2)$, midpoint = (__, __)

19) $(14, 13), (-4, 9)$, midpoint = (__, __)

20) $(10, -4), (8, 12)$, midpoint = (__, __)

Chapter 8: Lines and Slope

Finding Distance of Two Points

✍ **Find the distance of each pair of points.**

1) $(0, 9), (4, 6),$

    Distance = ____

2) $(-4, 6), (8, 11),$

    Distance = ____

3) $(-6, 1), (-3, 5),$

    Distance = ____

4) $(-3, 2), (3, 10),$

    Distance = ____

5) $(-5, 3), (4, -9),$

    Distance = ____

6) $(-7, -5), (5, 0),$

    Distance = ____

7) $(4, 3), (-4, -12),$

    Distance = ____

8) $(10, 1), (-5, -19),$

    Distance = ____

9) $(3, 3), (-1, 5),$

    Distance = ____

10) $(2, -1), (10, 5),$

    Distance = ____

11) $(-3, 7), (-1, 4),$

    Distance = ____

12) $(5, -2), (9, -5),$

    Distance = ____

13) $(-8, 4), (4, 9),$

    Distance = ____

14) $(6, 8), (6, -6),$

    Distance = ____

15) $(6, -6), (0, 2),$

    Distance = ____

16) $(-4, 10), (-4, 4),$

    Distance = ____

17) $(-7, -6), (-2, 6),$

    Distance = ____

18) $(11, 0), (3, 15),$

    Distance = ____

www.EffortlessMath.com

Chapter 8: Lines and Slope

Answers – Chapter 8

Finding Slope

1) 2
2) -6
3) -1
4) -2
5) 2
6) -8
7) -4
8) -9
9) -2
10) 9
11) $\frac{1}{2}$
12) $-\frac{2}{5}$
13) $\frac{1}{3}$
14) -1
15) $\frac{1}{3}$
16) $\frac{1}{3}$
17) 2
18) 1
19) -2
20) 2
21) -1
22) 2
23) 2
24) -3
25) 1
26) 1
27) 2
28) -1

Graphing Lines Using Slope–Intercept Form

1) $y = -x + 1$

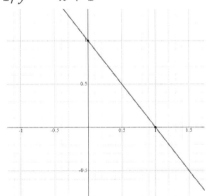

2) $y = 2x - 4$

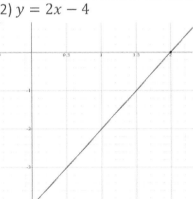

3) $y = -x + 6$

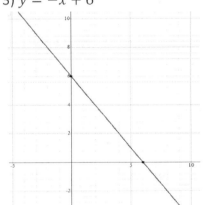

4) $y = x - 4$

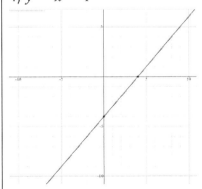

5) $y = 2x - 2$

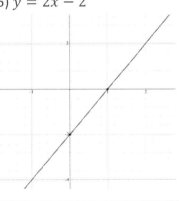

6) $y = -\frac{1}{2}x + 2$

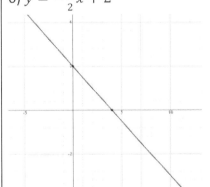

Chapter 8: Lines and Slope

Writing Linear Equations

1) $y = 6x - 14$
2) $y = x + 6$
3) $y = x + 4$
4) $y = x - 1$
5) $y = -4x + 18$
6) $y = x - 5$
7) $y = -x + 5$
8) $y = 7x + 22$
9) $y = x + 7$
10) $y = -7x + 50$
11) $y = 4x + 13$
12) $y = 4x - 24$
13) $y = -x + 3$
14) $y = -2x - 2$
15) $y = 9x - 44$
16) $y = -2x - 4$
17) $y = 6x + 4$
18) $y = 5x + 9$
19) $y = 8x - 8$
20) $y = -3x - 2$

Finding Midpoint

1) $midpoint = (2, 4)$
2) $midpoint = (2, 3)$
3) $midpoint = (2, 2)$
4) $midpoint = (-2, 4)$
5) $midpoint = (7, -4)$
6) $midpoint = (-1, -5)$
7) $midpoint = (0, 4)$
8) $midpoint = (-6, 2)$
9) $midpoint = (3, -1)$
10) $midpoint = (6, 1)$
11) $midpoint = (-1, 6)$
12) $midpoint = (3, -3)$
13) $midpoint = (-5, 9)$
14) $midpoint = (9, 2)$
15) $midpoint = (4, 5)$
16) $midpoint = (-7, 2)$
17) $midpoint = (9, 10)$
18) $midpoint = (3, -6)$
19) $midpoint = (5, 11)$
20) $midpoint = (9, 4)$

Chapter 8: Lines and Slope

Finding Distance of Two Points

1) Distance $= 5$

2) Distance $= 13$

3) Distance $= 5$

4) Distance $= 10$

5) Distance $= 15$

6) Distance $= 13$

7) Distance $= 17$

8) Distance $= 25$

9) Distance $= \sqrt{20} = 2\sqrt{5}$

10) Distance $= 10$

11) Distance $= \sqrt{13}$

12) Distance $= 5$

13) Distance $= 13$

14) Distance $= 14$

15) Distance $= 10$

16) Distance $= 6$

17) Distance $= 13$

18) Distance $= 17$

Chapter 9: Exponents and Variables

Math Topics that you'll learn in this Chapter:

- ✓ Multiplication Property of Exponents
- ✓ Division Property of Exponents
- ✓ Powers of Products and Quotients
- ✓ Zero and Negative Exponents
- ✓ Negative Exponents and Negative Bases
- ✓ Scientific Notation
- ✓ Radicals

Chapter 9: Exponents and Variables

Multiplication Property of Exponents

✎ Simplify and write the answer in exponential form.

1) $3 \times 3^2 =$

2) $4^3 \times 4 =$

3) $2^2 \times 2^2 =$

4) $6^2 \times 6^2 =$

5) $7^3 \times 7^2 \times 7 =$

6) $2 \times 2^2 \times 2^2 =$

7) $5^3 \times 5^2 \times 5 \times 5 =$

8) $2x \times x =$

9) $x^3 \times x^2 =$

10) $x^4 \times x^4 =$

11) $x^2 \times x^2 \times x^2 =$

12) $6x \times 6x =$

13) $2x^2 \times 2x^2 =$

14) $3x^2 \times x =$

15) $4x^4 \times 4x^4 \times 4x^4 =$

16) $2x^2 \times x^2 =$

17) $x^4 \times 3x =$

18) $x \times 2x^2 =$

19) $5x^4 \times 5x^4 =$

20) $2yx^2 \times 2x =$

21) $3x^4 \times y^2x^4 =$

22) $y^2x^3 \times y^5x^2 =$

23) $4yx^3 \times 2x^2y^3 =$

24) $6x^2 \times 6x^3y^4 =$

25) $3x^4y^5 \times 7x^2y^3 =$

26) $7x^2y^5 \times 9xy^3 =$

27) $7xy^4 \times 4x^3y^3 =$

28) $3x^5y^3 \times 8x^2y^3 =$

29) $6x \times y^5x^2 \times y^3 =$

30) $yx^3 \times 3y^3x^2 \times 2xy =$

31) $5yx^3 \times 4y^2x \times xy^3 =$

32) $6x^2 \times 3x^3y^4 \times 10yx^3 =$

Chapter 9: Exponents and Variables

Division Property of Exponents

✎ *Simplify and write the answer.*

1) $\dfrac{3^2}{3^3} =$

2) $\dfrac{2^6}{2^2} =$

3) $\dfrac{4^4}{4} =$

4) $\dfrac{5}{5^4} =$

5) $\dfrac{x}{x^3} =$

6) $\dfrac{3 \times 3^3}{3^2 \times 3^4} =$

7) $\dfrac{5^8}{5^3} =$

8) $\dfrac{5 \times 5^6}{5^2 \times 5^7} =$

9) $\dfrac{3^4 \times 3^7}{3^2 \times 3^8} =$

10) $\dfrac{5x}{10x^3} =$

11) $\dfrac{5x^3}{2x^5} =$

12) $\dfrac{18x^3}{14x^6} =$

13) $\dfrac{12x^3}{8xy^8} =$

14) $\dfrac{24xy^3}{4x^4y^2} =$

15) $\dfrac{21x^3y^9}{7xy^5} =$

16) $\dfrac{36x^2y^9}{4x^3} =$

17) $\dfrac{18x^3y^4}{10x^6y^8} =$

18) $\dfrac{16y^2x^{14}}{24yx^8} =$

19) $\dfrac{15x^4y}{9x^9y^2} =$

20) $\dfrac{7x^7y^2}{28x^5y^6} =$

Chapter 9: Exponents and Variables

Powers of Products and Quotients

✏️ *Simplify and write the answer.*

1) $(3^2)^2 =$

2) $(5^2)^3 =$

3) $(3 \times 3^3)^4 =$

4) $(6 \times 6^4)^2 =$

5) $(3^3 \times 3^2)^3 =$

6) $(5^4 \times 5^5)^2 =$

7) $(2 \times 2^4)^2 =$

8) $(2x^6)^2 =$

9) $(11x^5)^2 =$

10) $(4x^2y^4)^4 =$

11) $(2x^4y^4)^3 =$

12) $(3x^2y^2)^2 =$

13) $(3x^4y^3)^4 =$

14) $(2x^6y^8)^2 =$

15) $(12x^3x)^3 =$

16) $(5x^9x^6)^3 =$

17) $(5x^{10}y^3)^3 =$

18) $(14x^3x^3)^2 =$

19) $(3x^35x)^2 =$

20) $(10x^{11}y^3)^2 =$

21) $(9x^7y^5)^2 =$

22) $(4x^4y^6)^5 =$

23) $(3x4y^3)^2 =$

24) $\left(\dfrac{6x}{x^2}\right)^2 =$

25) $\left(\dfrac{x^5y^5}{x^2y^2}\right)^3 =$

26) $\left(\dfrac{24x}{4x^6}\right)^2 =$

27) $\left(\dfrac{x^5}{x^6y^2}\right)^2 =$

28) $\left(\dfrac{xy^3}{x^2y^5}\right)^3 =$

29) $\left(\dfrac{3xy^3}{x^4}\right)^2 =$

30) $\left(\dfrac{xy^5}{4xy^3}\right)^3 =$

Chapter 9: Exponents and Variables

Zero and Negative Exponents

✎ *Evaluate the following expressions.*

1) $2^{-1} =$

2) $3^{-2} =$

3) $0^{10} =$

4) $1^{-8} =$

5) $8^{-1} =$

6) $8^{-2} =$

7) $2^{-4} =$

8) $10^{-2} =$

9) $9^{-2} =$

10) $3^{-3} =$

11) $7^{-3} =$

12) $3^{-4} =$

13) $6^{-3} =$

14) $5^{-3} =$

15) $22^{-1} =$

16) $4^{-4} =$

17) $5^{-4} =$

18) $15^{-2} =$

19) $4^{-5} =$

20) $9^{-3} =$

21) $3^{-5} =$

22) $5^{-4} =$

23) $12^{-2} =$

24) $15^{-3} =$

25) $20^{-3} =$

26) $50^{-2} =$

27) $18^{-3} =$

28) $24^{-2} =$

29) $30^{-3} =$

30) $10^{-5} =$

31) $\left(\frac{1}{8}\right)^{-1} =$

32) $\left(\frac{1}{5}\right)^{-2} =$

33) $\left(\frac{1}{7}\right)^{-2} =$

34) $\left(\frac{2}{3}\right)^{-2} =$

35) $\left(\frac{1}{5}\right)^{-3} =$

36) $\left(\frac{3}{4}\right)^{-2} =$

37) $\left(\frac{2}{5}\right)^{-2} =$

38) $\left(\frac{1}{2}\right)^{-8} =$

39) $\left(\frac{2}{3}\right)^{-3} =$

40) $\left(\frac{3}{4}\right)^{-3} =$

41) $\left(\frac{5}{6}\right)^{-2} =$

42) $\left(\frac{6}{9}\right)^{-2} =$

Chapter 9: Exponents and Variables

Negative Exponents and Negative Bases

✎ *Simplify and write the answer.*

1) $-2^{-1} =$

2) $-4^{-2} =$

3) $-3^{-4} =$

4) $-x^{-5} =$

5) $2x^{-1} =$

6) $-4x^{-3} =$

7) $-12x^{-5} =$

8) $-5x^{-2}y^{-3} =$

9) $20x^{-4}y^{-1} =$

10) $14a^{-6}b^{-7} =$

11) $-12x^2y^{-3} =$

12) $-\dfrac{25}{x^{-6}} =$

13) $-\dfrac{2x}{y^{-4}} =$

14) $(-\dfrac{1}{3x})^{-2} =$

15) $(-\dfrac{3}{4x})^{-2} =$

16) $-\dfrac{9}{a^{-7}b^{-2}} =$

17) $-\dfrac{5x}{x^{-3}} =$

18) $-\dfrac{a^{-3}}{b^{-2}} =$

19) $-\dfrac{8}{x^{-3}} =$

20) $\dfrac{5b}{-9c^{-4}} =$

21) $\dfrac{9ab}{a^{-3}b^{-1}} =$

22) $-\dfrac{15a^{-2}}{30b^{-3}} =$

23) $\dfrac{4ab^{-2}}{-3c^{-2}} =$

24) $(\dfrac{3a}{2c})^{-2} =$

25) $(-\dfrac{3x}{4yz})^{-2} =$

26) $\dfrac{15ab^{-6}}{-9c^{-2}} =$

27) $(-\dfrac{x^3}{x^4})^{-3} =$

28) $(-\dfrac{x^{-2}}{2x^2})^{-2} =$

Chapter 9: Exponents and Variables

Scientific Notation

✎ *Write each number in scientific notation.*

1) $0.114 =$

2) $0.06 =$

3) $8.6 =$

4) $30 =$

5) $60 =$

6) $0.004 =$

7) $78 =$

8) $1,600 =$

9) $1,450 =$

10) $31,000 =$

11) $2,000,000 =$

12) $0.0000003 =$

13) $554,000 =$

14) $0.000725 =$

15) $0.00034 =$

16) $86,000,000 =$

17) $62,000 =$

18) $97,000,000 =$

19) $0.0000045 =$

20) $0.0019 =$

✎ *Write each number in standard notation.*

21) $2 \times 10^{-1} =$

22) $8 \times 10^{-2} =$

23) $1.8 \times 10^3 =$

24) $9 \times 10^{-4} =$

25) $1.7 \times 10^{-2} =$

26) $9 \times 10^3 =$

27) $6 \times 10^4 =$

28) $2.18 \times 10^5 =$

29) $5 \times 10^{-3} =$

30) $9.4 \times 10^{-5} =$

Chapter 9: Exponents and Variables

Radicals

✏️ *Simplify and write the answer.*

1) $\sqrt{1} =$ ____

2) $\sqrt{0} =$ ____

3) $\sqrt{16} =$ ____

4) $\sqrt{4} =$ ____

5) $\sqrt{9} =$ ____

6) $\sqrt{25} =$ ____

7) $\sqrt{49} =$ ____

8) $\sqrt{36} =$ ____

9) $\sqrt{64} =$ ____

10) $\sqrt{81} =$ ____

11) $\sqrt{121} =$ ____

12) $\sqrt{225} =$ ____

13) $\sqrt{144} =$ ____

14) $\sqrt{100} =$ ____

15) $\sqrt{256} =$ ____

16) $\sqrt{289} =$ ____

17) $\sqrt{324} =$ ____

18) $\sqrt{400} =$ ____

19) $\sqrt{900} =$ ____

20) $\sqrt{529} =$ ____

21) $\sqrt{361} =$ ____

22) $\sqrt{169} =$ ____

23) $\sqrt{196} =$ ____

24) $\sqrt{90} =$ ____

✏️ *Evaluate.*

25) $\sqrt{6} \times \sqrt{6} =$

26) $\sqrt{5} \times \sqrt{5} =$

27) $\sqrt{8} \times \sqrt{8} =$

28) $\sqrt{2} + \sqrt{2} =$

29) $\sqrt{8} + \sqrt{8} =$

30) $6\sqrt{5} - 2\sqrt{5} =$

31) $\sqrt{25} \times \sqrt{16} =$

32) $\sqrt{25} \times \sqrt{64} =$

33) $\sqrt{64} \times \sqrt{49} =$

34) $5\sqrt{5} \times 3\sqrt{5} =$

35) $7\sqrt{3} \times 2\sqrt{3} =$

36) $5\sqrt{2} - \sqrt{8} =$

Chapter 9: Exponents and Variables

Answers – Chapter 9

Multiplication Property of Exponents

1) 3^3
2) 4^4
3) 2^4
4) 6^4
5) 7^6
6) 2^5
7) 5^7
8) $2x^2$

9) x^5
10) x^8
11) x^6
12) $36x^2$
13) $4x^4$
14) $3x^3$
15) $64x^{12}$
16) $2x^4$

17) $3x^5$
18) $2x^3$
19) $25x^8$
20) $4x^3y$
21) $3x^8y^2$
22) x^5y^7
23) $8x^5y^4$
24) $36x^5y^4$

25) $21x^6y^8$
26) $63x^3y^8$
27) $28x^4y^7$
28) $24x^7y^6$
29) $6x^3y^8$
30) $6x^6y^5$
31) $20x^5y^6$
32) $180x^8y^5$

Division Property of Exponents

1) $\frac{1}{3}$
2) 2^4
3) 4^3
4) $\frac{1}{5^3}$
5) $\frac{1}{x^2}$

6) $\frac{1}{3^2}$
7) 5^5
8) $\frac{1}{5^2}$
9) 3
10) $\frac{1}{2x^2}$

11) $\frac{5}{2x^2}$
12) $\frac{9}{7x^3}$
13) $\frac{3x^2}{2y^8}$
14) $\frac{6y}{x^3}$
15) $3x^2y^4$

16) $\frac{9y^9}{x}$
17) $\frac{9}{5x^3y^4}$
18) $\frac{2yx^6}{3}$
19) $\frac{5}{3x^5y}$
20) $\frac{x^2}{4y^4}$

Chapter 9: Exponents and Variables

Powers of Products and Quotients

1) 3^4

2) 5^6

3) 3^{16}

4) 6^{10}

5) 3^{15}

6) 5^{18}

7) 2^{10}

8) $4x^{12}$

9) $121x^{10}$

10) $256x^8y^{16}$

11) $8x^{12}y^{12}$

12) $9x^4y^4$

13) $81x^{16}y^{12}$

14) $4x^{12}y^{16}$

15) $1,728x^{12}$

16) $125x^{45}$

17) $125x^{30}y^9$

18) $196x^{12}$

19) $225x^8$

20) $100x^{22}y^6$

21) $81x^{14}y^{10}$

22) $1,024x^{20}y^{30}$

23) $144x^2y^6$

24) $\dfrac{36}{x^2}$

25) x^9y^9

26) $\dfrac{36}{x^{10}}$

27) $\dfrac{1}{x^2y^4}$

28) $\dfrac{1}{x^3y^6}$

29) $\dfrac{9y^6}{x^6}$

30) $\dfrac{y^6}{64}$

Chapter 9: Exponents and Variables

Zero and Negative Exponents

1) $\dfrac{1}{2}$

2) $\dfrac{1}{9}$

3) 0

4) 1

5) $\dfrac{1}{8}$

6) $\dfrac{1}{64}$

7) $\dfrac{1}{16}$

8) $\dfrac{1}{100}$

9) $\dfrac{1}{81}$

10) $\dfrac{1}{27}$

11) $\dfrac{1}{343}$

12) $\dfrac{1}{81}$

13) $\dfrac{1}{216}$

14) $\dfrac{1}{125}$

15) $\dfrac{1}{22}$

16) $\dfrac{1}{256}$

17) $\dfrac{1}{625}$

18) $\dfrac{1}{225}$

19) $\dfrac{1}{1,024}$

20) $\dfrac{1}{729}$

21) $\dfrac{1}{243}$

22) $\dfrac{1}{625}$

23) $\dfrac{1}{144}$

24) $\dfrac{1}{3,375}$

25) $\dfrac{1}{8,000}$

26) $\dfrac{1}{2,500}$

27) $\dfrac{1}{5,832}$

28) $\dfrac{1}{576}$

29) $\dfrac{1}{27,000}$

30) $\dfrac{1}{100,000}$

31) 8

32) 25

33) 49

34) $\dfrac{9}{4}$

35) 125

36) $\dfrac{16}{9}$

37) $\dfrac{25}{4}$

38) 256

39) $\dfrac{27}{8}$

40) $\dfrac{64}{27}$

41) $\dfrac{36}{25}$

42) $\dfrac{81}{36}$

Chapter 9: Exponents and Variables

Negative Exponents and Negative Bases

1) $-\frac{1}{2}$

2) $-\frac{1}{16}$

3) $-\frac{1}{81}$

4) $-\frac{1}{x^5}$

5) $\frac{2}{x}$

6) $-\frac{4}{x^3}$

7) $-\frac{12}{x^5}$

8) $-\frac{5}{x^2y^3}$

9) $\frac{20}{x^4y}$

10) $\frac{14}{a^6b^7}$

11) $-\frac{12x^2}{y^3}$

12) $-25x^6$

13) $-2xy^4$

14) $9x^2$

15) $\frac{16x^2}{9}$

16) $-9a^7b^2$

17) $-5x^4$

18) $-\frac{b^2}{a^3}$

19) $-8x^3$

20) $-\frac{5bc^4}{9}$

21) $9a^4b^2$

22) $-\frac{b^3}{2a^2}$

23) $-\frac{4ac^2}{3b^2}$

24) $\frac{4c^2}{9a^2}$

25) $\frac{16y^2z^2}{9x^2}$

26) $-\frac{5ac^2}{3b^6}$

27) $-x^3$

28) $4x^8$

Chapter 9: Exponents and Variables

Scientific Notation

1) 1.14×10^{-1}

2) 6×10^{-2}

3) 8.6×10^0

4) 3×10^1

5) 6×10^1

6) 4×10^{-3}

7) 7.8×10^1

8) 1.6×10^3

9) 1.45×10^3

10) 3.1×10^4

11) 2×10^6

12) 3×10^{-7}

13) 5.54×10^5

14) 7.25×10^{-4}

15) 3.4×10^{-4}

16) 8.6×10^7

17) 6.2×10^4

18) 9.7×10^7

19) 4.5×10^{-6}

20) 1.9×10^{-3}

21) 0.2

22) 0.08

23) $1,800$

24) 0.0009

25) 0.017

26) $9,000$

27) $60,000$

28) $218,000$

29) 0.005

30) 0.000094

Chapter 9: Exponents and Variables

Radicals

1) 1
2) 0
3) 4
4) 2
5) 3
6) 5
7) 7
8) 6
9) 8
10) 9
11) 11
12) 15

13) 12
14) 10
15) 16
16) 17
17) 18
18) 20
19) 30
20) 23
21) 19
22) 13
23) 14
24) $3\sqrt{10}$

25) 6
26) 5
27) 8
28) $2\sqrt{2}$
29) $2\sqrt{8} = 4\sqrt{2}$
30) $4\sqrt{5}$
31) 20
32) 40
33) 56
34) 75
35) 42
36) $3\sqrt{2}$

Chapter 10: Polynomials

Math Topics that you'll learn in this Chapter:

- ✓ Simplifying Polynomials
- ✓ Adding and Subtracting Polynomials
- ✓ Multiplying Monomials
- ✓ Multiplying and Dividing Monomials
- ✓ Multiplying a Polynomial and a Monomial
- ✓ Multiplying Binomials
- ✓ Factoring Trinomials

Chapter 10: Polynomials

Simplifying Polynomials

Simplify each expression.

1) $3(2x + 1) =$ _____

2) $2(4x - 6) =$ _____

3) $4(3x + 3) =$ _____

4) $2(4x + 5) =$ _____

5) $-3(8x - 7) =$ _____

6) $2x(3x + 4) =$ _____

7) $3x^2 + 3x^2 - 2x^3 =$ _____

8) $2x - x^2 + 6x^3 + 4 =$ _____

9) $5x + 2x^2 - 9x^3 =$ _____

10) $7x^2 + 5x^4 - 2x^3 =$ _____

11) $-3x^2 + 5x^3 + 6x^4 =$ _____

12) $(x - 3)(x - 4) =$ _____

13) $(x - 5)(x + 4) =$ _____

14) $(x - 6)(x - 3) =$ _____

15) $(2x + 5)(x + 8) =$ _____

16) $(3x - 8)(x + 4) =$ _____

17) $-8x^2 + 2x^3 - 10x^4 + 5x =$ _____

18) $11 - 6x^2 + 5x^2 - 12x^3 + 22 =$ _____

19) $3x^2 - 4x + 4x^3 + 10x - 21x =$ _____

20) $10 - 6x^2 + 5x^2 - 3x^3 + 2 =$ _____

21) $3x^5 - 2x^3 + 8x^2 - x^5 =$ _____

22) $(5x^3 - 1) + (4x^3 - 6x^3) =$ _____

Chapter 10: Polynomials

Adding and Subtracting Polynomials

✏️ *Add or subtract expressions.*

1) $(x^2 - 5) + (x^2 + 6) =$ _____

2) $(2x^2 - 6) - (3 - 2x^2) =$ _____

3) $(x^3 + 3x^2) - (x^3 + 6) =$ _____

4) $(4x^3 - x^2) + (6x^2 - 8x) =$ _____

5) $(2x^3 + 3x) - (5x^3 + 2) =$ _____

6) $(5x^3 - 2) + (2x^3 + 10) =$ _____

7) $(7x^3 + 5) - (9 - 4x^3) =$ _____

8) $(5x^2 + 3x^3) - (2x^3 + 6) =$ _____

9) $(8x^2 - x) + (4x - 8x^2) =$ _____

10) $(6x + 9x^2) - (5x + 2) =$ _____

11) $(7x^4 - 2x) - (6x - 2x^4) =$ _____

12) $(2x - 4x^3) - (9x^3 + 6x) =$ _____

13) $(8x^3 - 8x^2) - (6x^2 - 3x) =$ _____

14) $(9x^2 - 6) + (5x^2 - 4x^3) =$ _____

15) $(8x^3 + 3x^4) - (x^4 - 3x^3) =$ _____

16) $(-4x^3 - 2x) + (5x - 2x^3) =$ _____

17) $(9x - 5x^4) - (8x^4 + 4x) =$ _____

18) $(8x - 3x^2) - (7x^4 - 3x^2) =$ _____

19) $(9x^3 - 7) + (5x^3 - 4x^2) =$ _____

20) $(7x^3 + x^4) - (6x^4 - 5x^3) =$ _____

Chapter 10: Polynomials

Multiplying Monomials

✏️ *Simplify each expression.*

1) $4x^7 \times x^3 =$

2) $6y^2 \times 6y^3 =$

3) $-6z^7 \times 4z^4 =$

4) $5x^5y \times 8xy^3 =$

5) $-6xy^8 \times 3x^5y^3 =$

6) $7a^4b^2 \times 3a^8b =$

7) $5xy^5 \times 3x^3y^4 =$

8) $5p^5q^4 \times (-6pq^4) =$

9) $8s^6t^2 \times 6s^3t^7 =$

10) $(-8x^5y^2) \times 4x^6y^3 =$

11) $9xy^6z \times 3y^4z^2 =$

12) $12x^5y^4 \times 2x^8y =$

13) $4pq^5 \times (-7p^4q^8) =$

14) $9s^4t^2 \times (-5st^5) =$

15) $10p^3q^5 \times (-4p^4q^6) =$

16) $(-5p^2q^4r) \times 7pq^5r^3 =$

17) $(-9a^4b^7c^4) \times (-4a^7b) =$

18) $7u^5v^9 \times (-5u^{12}v^7) =$

19) $4u^4v^9z^2 \times (-5uv^8z) =$

20) $(-6xy^3z^5) \times 3x^3yz^7 =$

21) $6x^2y^3z^5 \times (-7x^4y^2z) =$

22) $7a^5b^8c^{12} \times 4a^6b^5c^9 =$

Chapter 10: Polynomials

Multiplying and Dividing Monomials

✎ **Simplify each expression.**

1) $(3x^5)(2x^2) =$

2) $(6x^5)(2x^4) =$

3) $(-7x^9)(2x^5) =$

4) $(7x^7y^9)(-5x^6y^6) =$

5) $(8x^5y^6)(3x^2y^5) =$

6) $(8yx^2)(7y^5x^3) =$

7) $(4x^2y)(2x^2y^3) =$

8) $(-2x^9y^4)(-9x^6y^8) =$

9) $(-5x^8y^2)(-6x^4y^5) =$

10) $(8x^8y)(-7x^4y^3) =$

11) $(9x^6y^2)(6x^7y^4) =$

12) $(8x^9y^5)(6x^5y^4) =$

13) $(-5x^8y^9)(7x^7y^8) =$

14) $(6x^2y^5)(5x^3y^2) =$

15) $(9x^5y^{12})(4x^7y^9) =$

16) $(-10x^{14}y^8)(2x^7y^5) =$

17) $\frac{6x^5y^7}{xy^6} =$

18) $\frac{9x^6y^6}{3x^4y} =$

19) $\frac{16x^4y^6}{4xy} =$

20) $\frac{-30x^9y^8}{5x^5y^4} =$

Chapter 10: Polynomials

Multiplying a Polynomial and a Monomial

Find each product.

1) $x(x - 5) =$

2) $2(3 + x) =$

3) $x(x - 7) =$

4) $x(x + 9) =$

5) $2x(x - 2) =$

6) $5(4x + 3) =$

7) $4x(3x - 4) =$

8) $x(5x + 2y) =$

9) $3x(x - 2y) =$

10) $6x(3x - 4y) =$

11) $2x(3x - 8) =$

12) $6x(4x - 6y) =$

13) $3x(4x - 2y) =$

14) $2x(2x - 6y) =$

15) $5x(x^2 + y^2) =$

16) $3x(2x^2 - y^2) =$

17) $6(9x^2 + 3y^2) =$

18) $4x(-3x^2y + 2y) =$

19) $-3(6x^2 - 5xy + 3) =$

20) $6(x^2 - 4xy - 3) =$

www.EffortlessMath.com

Chapter 10: Polynomials

Multiplying Binomials

✎ *Find each product.*

1) $(x-3)(x+4) =$

2) $(x+3)(x+5) =$

3) $(x-6)(x-7) =$

4) $(x-9)(x-4) =$

5) $(x-7)(x-5) =$

6) $(x+6)(x+2) =$

7) $(x-9)(x+3) =$

8) $(x-8)(x-5) =$

9) $(x+3)(x+7) =$

10) $(x-9)(x+4) =$

11) $(x+6)(x+6) =$

12) $(x+7)(x+7) =$

13) $(x-8)(x+7) =$

14) $(x+9)(x+9) =$

15) $(x-8)(x-8) =$

16) $(x-9)(x+5) =$

17) $(2x-5)(x+4) =$

18) $(2x+6)(x+3) =$

19) $(2x+4)(x+5) =$

20) $(2x-3)(2x+2) =$

Chapter 10: Polynomials

Factoring Trinomials

Factor each trinomial.

1) $x^2 + 5x + 4 =$

2) $x^2 + 5x + 6 =$

3) $x^2 - 4x + 3 =$

4) $x^2 - 10x + 25 =$

5) $x^2 - 13x + 40 =$

6) $x^2 + 8x + 12 =$

7) $x^2 - 6x - 27 =$

8) $x^2 - 14x + 48 =$

9) $x^2 + 15x + 56 =$

10) $x^2 - 5x - 36 =$

11) $x^2 + 12x + 36 =$

12) $x^2 + 16x + 63 =$

13) $x^2 + x - 72 =$

14) $x^2 + 18x + 81 =$

15) $x^2 - 16x + 64 =$

16) $x^2 - 18x + 81 =$

17) $2x^2 + 10x + 8 =$

18) $2x^2 + 4x - 6 =$

19) $2x^2 + 9x + 4 =$

20) $4x^2 + 4x - 24 =$

Chapter 10: Polynomials

Answers – Chapter 10

Simplifying Polynomials

1) $6x + 3$

2) $8x - 12$

3) $12x + 12$

4) $8x + 10$

5) $-24x + 21$

6) $6x^2 + 8x$

7) $-2x^3 + 6x^2$

8) $6x^3 - x^2 + 2x + 4$

9) $-9x^3 + 2x^2 + 5x$

10) $5x^4 - 2x^3 + 7x^2$

11) $6x^4 + 5x^3 - 3x^2$

12) $x^2 - 7x + 12$

13) $x^2 - x - 20$

14) $x^2 - 9x + 18$

15) $2x^2 + 21x + 40$

16) $3x^2 + 4x - 32$

17) $-10x^4 + 2x^3 - 8x^2 + 5x$

18) $-12x^3 - x^2 + 33$

19) $4x^3 + 3x^2 - 15x$

20) $-3x^3 - x^2 + 12$

21) $2x^5 - 2x^3 + 8x^2$

22) $3x^3 - 1$

Chapter 10: Polynomials

Adding and Subtracting Polynomials

1) $2x^2 + 1$
2) $4x^2 - 9$
3) $3x^2 - 6$
4) $4x^3 + 5x^2 - 8x$
5) $-3x^3 + 3x - 2$
6) $7x^3 + 8$
7) $11x^3 - 4$
8) $x^3 + 5x^2 - 6$
9) $3x$
10) $9x^2 + x - 2$
11) $9x^4 - 8x$
12) $-13x^3 - 4x$
13) $8x^3 - 14x^2 + 3x$
14) $-4x^3 + 14x^2 - 6$
15) $2x^4 + 11x^3$
16) $-6x^3 + 3x$
17) $-13x^4 + 5x$
18) $-7x^4 + 8x$
19) $14x^3 - 4x^2 - 7$
20) $-5x^4 + 12x^3$

Multiplying Monomials

1) $4x^{10}$
2) $36y^5$
3) $-24z^{11}$
4) $40x^6y^4$
5) $-18x^6y^{11}$
6) $21a^{12}b^3$
7) $15x^4y^9$
8) $-30p^6q^8$
9) $48s^9t^9$
10) $-32x^{11}y^5$
11) $27xy^{10}z^3$
12) $24x^{13}y^5$
13) $-28p^5q^{13}$
14) $-45s^5t^7$
15) $-40p^7q^{11}$
16) $-35p^3q^9r^4$
17) $36a^{11}b^8c^4$
18) $-35u^{17}v^{16}$
19) $-20u^5v^{17}z^3$
20) $-18x^4y^4z^{12}$
21) $-42x^6y^5z^6$
22) $28a^{11}b^{13}c^{21}$

Chapter 10: Polynomials

Multiplying and Dividing Monomials

1) $6x^7$
2) $12x^9$
3) $-14x^{14}$
4) $-35x^{13}y^{15}$
5) $24x^7y^{11}$
6) $56y^6x^5$
7) $8x^4y^4$
8) $18x^{15}y^{12}$
9) $30x^{12}y^7$
10) $-56x^{12}y^4$
11) $54x^{13}y^6$
12) $48x^{14}y^9$
13) $-35x^{15}y^{17}$
14) $30x^5y^7$
15) $36x^{12}y^{21}$
16) $-20x^{21}y^{13}$
17) $6x^4y$
18) $3x^2y^5$
19) $4x^3y^5$
20) $-6x^4y^4$

Multiplying a Polynomial and a Monomial

1) $x^2 - 5x$
2) $2x + 6$
3) $x^2 - 7x$
4) $x^2 + 9x$
5) $2x^2 - 4x$
6) $20x + 15$
7) $12x^2 - 16x$
8) $5x^2 + 2xy$
9) $3x^2 - 6xy$
10) $18x^2 - 24xy$
11) $6x^2 - 16x$
12) $24x^2 - 36xy$
13) $12x^2 - 6xy$
14) $4x^2 - 12xy$
15) $5x^3 + 5xy^2$
16) $6x^3 - 3xy^2$
17) $54x^2 + 18y^2$
18) $-12x^3y + 8xy$
19) $-18x^2 + 15xy - 9$
20) $6x^2 - 24xy - 18$

Chapter 10: Polynomials

Multiplying Binomials

1) $x^2 + x - 12$

2) $x^2 + 8x + 15$

3) $x^2 - 13x + 42$

4) $x^2 - 13x + 36$

5) $x^2 - 12x + 35$

6) $x^2 + 8x + 12$

7) $x^2 - 6x - 27$

8) $x^2 - 13x + 40$

9) $x^2 + 10x + 21$

10) $x^2 - 5x - 36$

11) $x^2 + 12x + 36$

12) $x^2 + 14x + 49$

13) $x^2 - x - 56$

14) $x^2 + 18x + 81$

15) $x^2 - 16x + 64$

16) $x^2 - 4x - 45$

17) $2x^2 + 3x - 20$

18) $2x^2 + 12x + 18$

19) $2x^2 + 14x + 20$

20) $4x^2 - 2x - 6$

Chapter 10: Polynomials

Factoring Trinomials

1) $(x+4)(x+1)$

2) $(x+3)(x+2)$

3) $(x-1)(x-3)$

4) $(x-5)(x-5)$

5) $(x-8)(x-5)$

6) $(x+6)(x+2)$

7) $(x-9)(x+3)$

8) $(x-8)(x-6)$

9) $(x+8)(x+7)$

10) $(x-9)(x+4)$

11) $(x+6)(x+6)$

12) $(x+7)(x+9)$

13) $(x-8)(x+9)$

14) $(x+9)(x+9)$

15) $(x-8)(x-8)$

16) $(x-9)(x-9)$

17) $2(x+1)(x+4)$

18) $2(x-1)(x+3)$

19) $(2x+1)(x+4)$

20) $(2x-4)(2x+6)$

Chapter 11: Geometry and Solid Figures

Math Topics that you'll learn in this Chapter:

- ✓ The Pythagorean Theorem
- ✓ Triangles
- ✓ Polygons
- ✓ Circles
- ✓ Trapezoids
- ✓ Cubes
- ✓ Rectangle Prisms
- ✓ Cylinder

Chapter 11: Geometry and Solid Figures

The Pythagorean Theorem

🖉 **Do the following lengths form a right triangle?**

1) _____

2) _____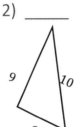

3) _____

4) _____

5) _____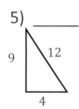

6) _____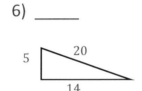

7) _____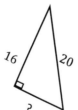

8) _____

🖉 **Find the missing side.**

9) _____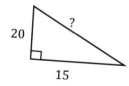

10) _____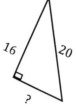

11) _____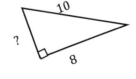

12) _____

13) _____

14) _____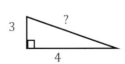

15) _____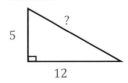

16) _____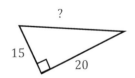

106

www.EffortlessMath.com

Chapter 11: Geometry and Solid Figures

Triangles

✎ **Find the measure of the unknown angle in each triangle.**

1) _____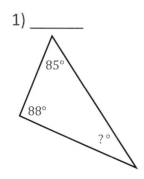

2) _____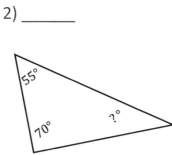

3) _____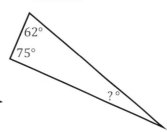

4) _____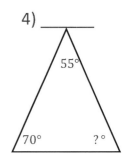

5) _____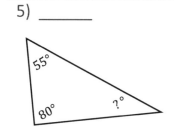

6) _____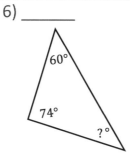

7) _____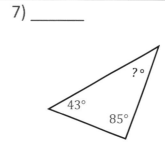

8) _____

✎ **Find area of each triangle.**

9) _____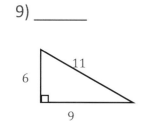

10) _____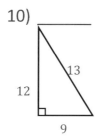

11) _____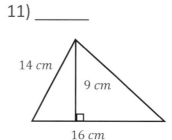

12) _____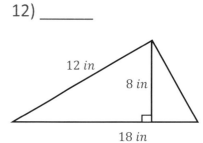

Chapter 11: Geometry and Solid Figures

Polygons

🖉 *Find the perimeter of each shape.*

1) (square) _____   2) _____   3) _____   4) (square) _____

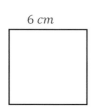
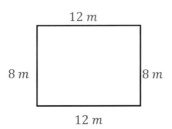
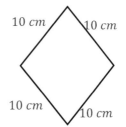
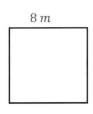

5) (regular hexagon) _____   6) _____   7) (parallelogram) _____   8) (regular hexagon) _____

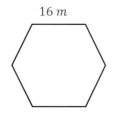
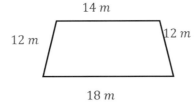
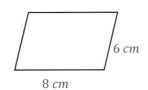
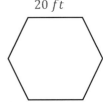

9) _____   10) _____   11) _____   12) (regular hexagon) _____

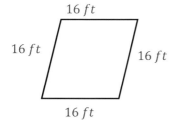
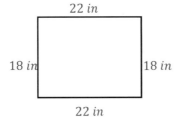
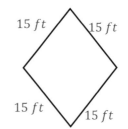
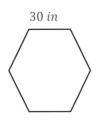

Chapter 11: Geometry and Solid Figures

Circles

✏️ **Find the Circumference of each circle.** (π = 3.14)

1) ____ 2) ____ 3) ____ 4) ____ 5) ____ 6) ____

7) ____ 8) ____ 9) ____ 10) ____ 11) ____ 12) ____

✏️ **Complete the table below.** (π = 3.14)

	Radius	Diameter	Circumference	Area
Circle 1	2 inches	4 inches	12.56 inches	12.56 square inches
Circle 2		8 meters		
Circle 3				113.04 square feet
Circle 4			50.24 miles	
Circle 5		9 kilometers		
Circle 6	7 centimeters			
Circle 7		18 feet		
Circle 8				78.5 square meters
Circle 9			69.08 inches	
Circle 10	10 feet			

Chapter 11: Geometry and Solid Figures

Cubes

✏️ Find the volume of each cube.

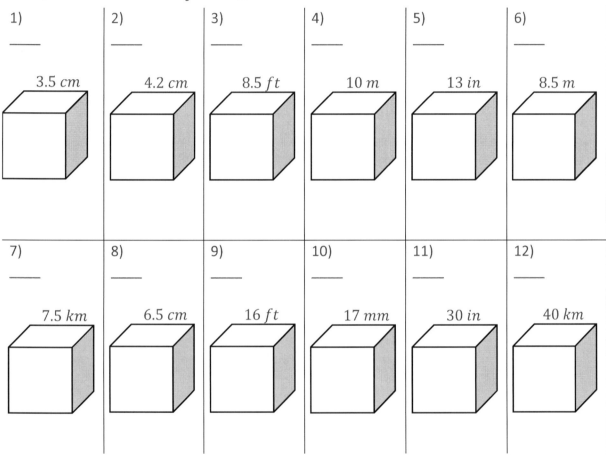

1) 3.5 cm
2) 4.2 cm
3) 8.5 ft
4) 10 m
5) 13 in
6) 8.5 m
7) 7.5 km
8) 6.5 cm
9) 16 ft
10) 17 mm
11) 30 in
12) 40 km

✏️ Find the surface area of each cube.

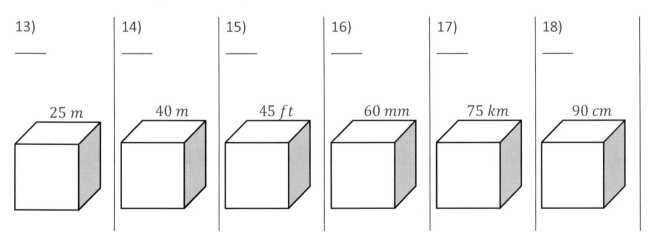

13) 25 m
14) 40 m
15) 45 ft
16) 60 mm
17) 75 km
18) 90 cm

Chapter 11: Geometry and Solid Figures

Trapezoids

✏️ *Find the area of each trapezoid.*

1) _____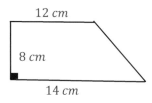

2) _____

3) _____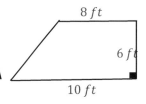

4) _____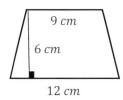

5) _____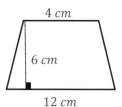

6) _____

7) _____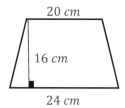

8) _____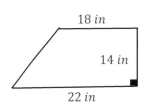

✏️ *Solve.*

9) A trapezoid has an area of 78 cm^2 and its height is 10 cm and one base is 8 cm. What is the other base length? _____

10) If a trapezoid has an area of 160 ft^2 and the lengths of the bases are 12 ft and 8 ft, find the height. _____

11) If a trapezoid has an area of 180 m^2 and its height is 8 m and one base is 10 m, find the other base length. _____

12) The area of a trapezoid is 150 ft^2 and its height is 20 ft. If one base of the trapezoid is 12 ft, what is the other base length? _____

Chapter 11: Geometry and Solid Figures

Rectangular Prisms

✏️ **Find the volume of each Rectangular Prism.**

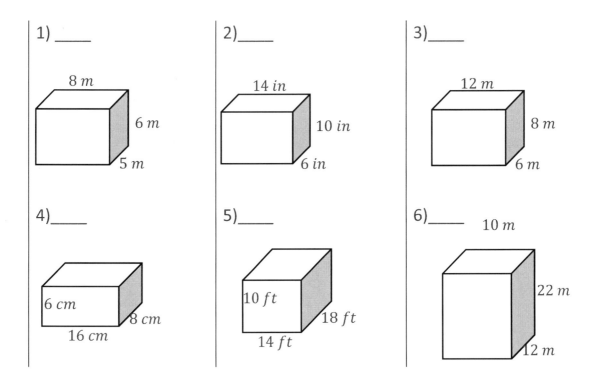

✏️ **Find the surface area of each Rectangular Prism.**

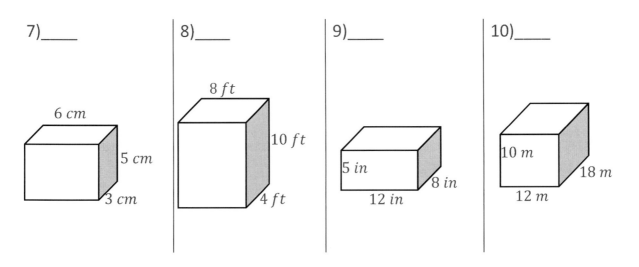

Chapter 11: Geometry and Solid Figures

Cylinder

✎ **Find the volume of each Cylinder.** (π = 3.14)

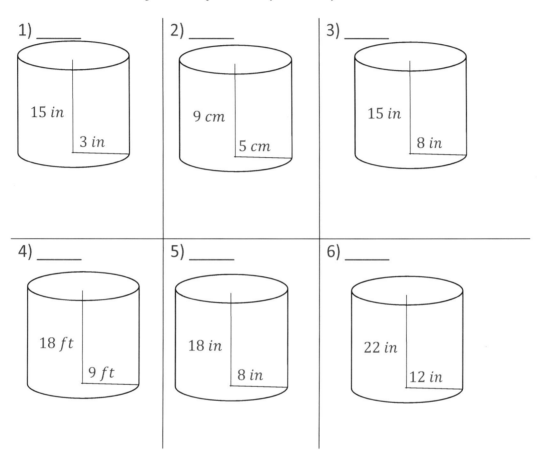

1) _____ (15 in, 3 in)
2) _____ (9 cm, 5 cm)
3) _____ (15 in, 8 in)
4) _____ (18 ft, 9 ft)
5) _____ (18 in, 8 in)
6) _____ (22 in, 12 in)

✎ **Find the surface area of each Cylinder.** (π = 3.14)

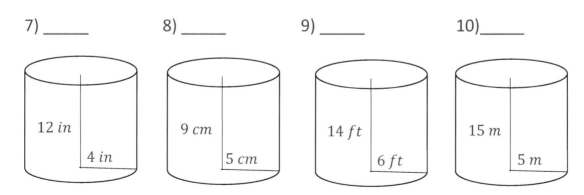

7) _____ (12 in, 4 in)
8) _____ (9 cm, 5 cm)
9) _____ (14 ft, 6 ft)
10) _____ (15 m, 5 m)

Chapter 11: Geometry and Solid Figures

Answers – Chapter 11

The Pythagorean Theorem

1) no
2) no
3) no
4) yes
5) no
6) no
7) yes
8) yes
9) 25
10) 12
11) 6
12) 34
13) 10
14) 5
15) 13
16) 25

Triangles

1) 7°
2) 55°
3) 43°
4) 55°
5) 45°
6) 46°
7) 52°
8) 71°
9) 27
10) 54
11) 72 cm^2
12) 72 in^2

Polygons

1) 24 cm
2) 40 m
3) 40 cm
4) 32 m
5) 96 m
6) 56 m
7) 28 cm
8) 120 ft
9) 64 ft
10) 80 in
11) 60 ft
12) 180 in

Chapter 11: Geometry and Solid Figures

Circles

1) 37.68 *in*
2) 62.8 *cm*
3) 119.32 *ft*
4) 75.36 *m*
5) 113.04 *cm*
6) 94.2 *miles*
7) 119.32 *in*
8) 138.16 *ft*
9) 157 *m*
10) 175.84 *m*
11) 219.8 *in*
12) 314 *ft*

	Radius	Diameter	Circumference	Area
Circle 1	2 inches	4 inches	12.56 inches	12.56 square inches
Circle 2	4 meters	8 meters	25.12 meters	50.24 square meters
Circle 3	6 feet	12 feet	37.68 feet	113.04 square feet
Circle 4	8 miles	16 miles	50.24 miles	200.96 square miles
Circle 5	4.5 kilometers	9 kilometers	28.26 kilometers	63.585 square kilometers
Circle 6	7 centimeters	14 centimeters	43.96 centimeters	153.86 square centimeters
Circle 7	9 feet	18 feet	56.52 feet	254.34 square feet
Circle 8	5 meters	10 meters	31.4 meters	78.5 square meters
Circle 9	11 inches	22 inches	69.08 inches	379.94 square inches
Circle 10	10 feet	20 feet	62.8 feet	314 square feet

Cubes

1) $42.875\ cm^3$
2) $74.088\ cm^3$
3) $614.125\ ft^3$
4) $1,000\ m^3$
5) $2,197\ in^3$
6) $614.125\ m^3$
7) $421.875\ km^3$
8) $274.625\ cm^3$
9) $4,096\ ft^3$
10) $4,913\ mm^3$
11) $27,000\ in^3$
12) $64,000\ km^3$
13) $3,750\ m^2$
14) $9,600\ m^2$
15) $12,150\ ft^2$
16) $21,600\ mm^2$
17) $33,750\ km^2$
18) $48,600\ cm^2$

Chapter 11: Geometry and Solid Figures

Trapezoids

1) $104 \ cm^2$
2) $216 \ m^2$
3) $54 \ ft^2$
4) $63 \ cm^2$
5) $48 \ cm^2$
6) $112 \ in^2$
7) $352 \ cm^2$
8) $280 \ in^2$
9) $7.6 \ cm$
10) $16 \ ft$
11) $35 \ m$
12) $3 \ ft$

Rectangular Prisms

1) $240 \ m^3$
2) $840 \ in^3$
3) $576 \ m^3$
4) $768 \ cm^3$
5) $2,520 \ ft^3$
6) $2,640 \ m^3$
7) $126 \ cm^2$
8) $304 \ ft^2$
9) $392 \ in^2$
10) $1,032 \ m^2$

Cylinder

1) $423.9 \ in^3$
2) $706.5 \ cm^3$
3) $3,014.4 \ in^3$
4) $4,578.12 \ ft^3$
5) $3,617.28 \ in^3$
6) $9,947.52 \ in^3$
7) $401.92 \ in^2$
8) $439.6 \ cm^2$
9) $753.6 \ ft^2$
10) $628 \ m^2$

Chapter 12: Statistics

Math Topics that you'll learn in this Chapter:

- ✓ Mean, Median, Mode, and Range of the Given Data
- ✓ Pie Graph
- ✓ Probability Problems
- ✓ Permutations and Combinations

Chapter 12: Statistics

Mean, Median, Mode, and Range of the Given Data

✎ **Find the values of the Given Data.**

1) 5, 12, 2, 2, 6

   Mode: _____   Range: _____

   Mean: _____   Median: _____

2) 5, 9, 3, 6, 4, 3

   Mode: _____   Range: _____

   Mean: _____   Median: _____

3) 12, 5, 8, 7, 8

   Mode: _____   Range: _____

   Mean: _____   Median: _____

4) 9, 7, 12, 7, 3, 4

   Mode: _____   Range: _____

   Mean: _____   Median: _____

5) 9, 7, 10, 5, 7, 4, 14

   Mode: _____   Range: _____

   Mean: _____   Median: _____

6) 8, 1, 6, 6, 9, 2, 17

   Mode: _____   Range: _____

   Mean: _____   Median: _____

7) 14, 5, 2, 7, 10, 7, 8, 13

   Mode: _____   Range: _____

   Mean: _____   Median: _____

8) 12, 14, 6, 4, 10, 8, 2

   Mode: _____   Range: _____

   Mean: _____   Median: _____

9) 17, 13, 16, 12, 14, 24

   Mode: _____   Range: _____

   Mean: _____   Median: _____

10) 18, 15, 10, 8, 4, 7, 8, 18

   Mode: _____   Range: _____

   Mean: _____   Median: _____

Chapter 12: Statistics

Pie Graph

✎ **The circle graph below shows all Wilson's expenses for last month. Wilson spent** $300 **on his bills last month.**

Answer following questions based on the Pie graph.

Wilson's last month expenses

- Clothes 30%
- Books 10%
- Others 28%
- Bills 12%
- Foods 20%

1) How much was Wilson's total expenses last month? _____

2) How much did Wilson spend on his clothes last month? _____

3) How much did Wilson spend for foods last month? _____

4) How much did Wilson spend on his books last month? _____

5) What fraction is Wilson's expenses for his bills and clothes out of his total expenses last month? _____

Chapter 12: Statistics

Probability Problems

1) If there are 15 red balls and 30 blue balls in a basket, what is the probability that Oliver will pick out a red ball from the basket? _____

Gender	Under 45	45 or older	Total
Male	12	6	18
Female	5	7	12
Total	17	13	30

2) The table above shows the distribution of age and gender for 30 employees in a company. If one employee is selected at random, what is the probability that the employee selected be either a female under age 45 or a male age 45 or older? _____

3) A number is chosen at random from 1 to 18. Find the probability of not selecting a composite number. (A composite number is a number that is divisible by itself, 1 and at least one other whole number) _____

4) There are 6 blue marbles, 8 red marbles, and 5 yellow marbles in a box. If Ava randomly selects a marble from the box, what is the probability of selecting a red or yellow marble? _____

5) A bag contains 20 balls: three green, six black, eight blue, a brown, a red and one white. If 19 balls are removed from the bag at random, what is the probability that a brown ball has been removed? _____

6) There are only red and blue marbles in a box. The probability of choosing a red marble in the box at random is one third. If there are 160 blue marbles, how many marbles are in the box? _____

Chapter 12: Statistics

Permutations and Combinations

✎ *Calculate the value of each.*

1) $5! =$ ____

2) $6! =$ ____

3) $8! =$ ____

4) $5! + 6! =$ ____

5) $8! + 3! =$ ____

6) $6! + 7! =$ ____

7) $8! + 4! =$ ____

8) $9! - 3! =$ ____

✎ *Solve each word problems.*

9) Sophia is baking cookies. She uses milk, flour and eggs. How many different orders of ingredients can she try? _____

10) William is planning for his vacation. He wants to go to restaurant, watch a movie, go to the beach, and play basketball. How many different ways of ordering are there for him? _____

11) How many 7 —digit numbers can be named using the digits 1, 2, 3, 4, 5, 6 and 7 without repetition? _____

12) In how many ways can 9 boys be arranged in a straight line? _____

13) In how many ways can 8 athletes be arranged in a straight line? _____

14) A professor is going to arrange her 6 students in a straight line. In how many ways can she do this? _____

15) How many code symbols can be formed with the letters for the word BLUE? _____

16) In how many ways a team of 8 basketball players can choose a captain and co-captain? _____

Chapter 12: Statistics

Answers – Chapter 12

Mean, Median, Mode, and Range of the Given Data

1) Mode: 2   Range: 10   Mean: 5.4   Median: 5

2) Mode: 3   Range: 6   Mean: 5   Median: 4.5

3) Mode: 8   Range: 7   Mean: 8   Median: 8

4) Mode: 7   Range: 9   Mean: 7   Median: 7

5) Mode: 7   Range: 10   Mean: 8   Median: 7

6) Mode: 6   Range: 16   Mean: 7   Median: 6

7) Mode: 7   Range: 12   Mean: 8.25   Median: 7.5

8) Mode: *no mode*   Range: 12   Mean: 8   Median: 8

9) Mode: *no mode*   Range: 12   Mean: 16   Median: 15

10) Mode: 8,18   Range: 14   Mean: 11   Median: 9

Pie Graph

1) $2,500

2) $750

3) $500

4) $250

5) $\frac{21}{50}$

Chapter 12: Statistics

Probability Problems

1) $\frac{1}{3}$

2) $\frac{11}{30}$

3) $\frac{7}{18}$

4) $\frac{13}{19}$

5) $\frac{19}{20}$

6) 240

Permutations and Combinations

1) 120

2) 720

3) 40,320

4) 840

5) 40,326

6) 5,760

7) 40,344

8) 362,874

9) 6

10) 24

11) 5,040

12) 362,880

13) 40,320

14) 720

15) 24

16) 56

Chapter 13: Functions Operations

Math Topics that you'll learn in this Chapter:

- ✓ Function Notation and Evaluation
- ✓ Adding and Subtracting Functions
- ✓ Multiplying and Dividing Functions
- ✓ Composition of Functions

Chapter 13: Functions Operations

Function Notation and Evaluation

✏️ Evaluate each function.

1) $f(x) = x - 3$, find $f(-2)$

2) $g(x) = x + 5$, find $g(6)$

3) $h(x) = x + 8$, find $h(2)$

4) $f(x) = -x - 7$, find $f(5)$

5) $f(x) = 2x - 7$, find $f(-1)$

6) $w(x) = -2 - 4x$, find $w(5)$

7) $g(n) = 6n - 3$, find $g(-2)$

8) $h(x) = -8x + 12$, find $h(3)$

9) $k(n) = 14 - 3n$, find $k(3)$

10) $g(x) = 4x - 4$, find $g(-2)$

11) $k(n) = 8n - 7$, find $k(4)$

12) $w(n) = -2n + 14$, find $w(5)$

13) $h(x) = 5x - 18$, find $h(8)$

14) $g(n) = 2n^2 + 2$, find $g(5)$

15) $f(x) = 3x^2 - 13$, find $f(2)$

16) $g(n) = 5n^2 + 7$, find $g(-3)$

17) $h(n) = 5n^2 - 10$, find $h(4)$

18) $g(x) = -3x^2 - 6x$, find $g(2)$

19) $k(n) = 4n^3 + n$, find $k(-5)$

20) $f(x) = -3x + 10$, find $f(3x)$

21) $k(a) = 4a + 9$, find $k(a - 1)$

22) $h(x) = 8x + 4$, find $h(5x)$

Chapter 13: Functions Operations

Adding and Subtracting Functions

✍ **Perform the indicated operation.**

1) $f(x) = x + 4$
   $g(x) = 2x + 5$
   Find $(f - g)(2)$

   _____

2) $g(x) = x - 2$
   $f(x) = -x - 6$
   Find $(g - f)(-2)$

   _____

3) $h(t) = 4t + 4$
   $g(t) = 3t + 2$
   Find $(h + g)(-1)$

   _____

4) $g(a) = 5a - 7$
   $f(a) = a^2 + 3$
   Find $(g + f)(2)$

   _____

5) $g(x) = 4x - 5$
   $f(x) = 6x^2 + 5$
   Find $(g - f)(-2)$

   _____

6) $h(x) = x^2 + 3$
   $g(x) = -4x + 1$
   Find $(h + g)(4)$

   _____

7) $f(x) = -3x - 9$
   $g(x) = x^2 + 5$
   Find $(f - g)(6)$

   _____

8) $h(n) = -4n^2 + 9$
   $g(n) = 5n + 6$
   Find $(h - g)(5)$

   _____

9) $g(x) = 4x^2 - 3x - 1$
   $f(x) = 6x + 10$
   Find $(g - f)(a)$

   _____

10) $g(t) = -6t - 7$
    $f(t) = -t^2 + 3t + 15$
    Find $(g + f)(t)$

    _____

Chapter 13: Functions Operations

Multiplying and Dividing Functions

✎ *Perform the indicated operation.*

1) $g(x) = x + 6$
   $f(x) = x + 4$
   Find $(g.f)(2)$

2) $f(x) = 3x$
   $h(x) = -x + 5$
   Find $(f.h)(-2)$

3) $g(a) = a + 5$
   $h(a) = 2a - 4$
   Find $(g.h)(4)$

4) $f(x) = 3x + 2$
   $h(x) = 2x - 3$
   Find $(\frac{f}{h})(2)$

5) $f(x) = a^2 - 2$
   $g(x) = -4 + 3a$
   Find $(\frac{f}{g})(2)$

6) $g(a) = 4a + 6$
   $f(a) = 2a - 8$
   Find $(\frac{g}{f})(3)$

7) $g(t) = t^2 + 6$
   $h(t) = 2t - 3$
   Find $(g.h)(-3)$

8) $g(x) = x^2 + 3x + 4$
   $h(x) = 2x + 6$
   Find $(g.h)(2)$

9) $g(a) = 2a^2 - 5a + 1$
   $f(a) = 2a^3 - 6$
   Find $(\frac{g}{f})(4)$

10) $g(x) = -3x^2 + 4 - 2x$
    $f(x) = x^2 - 5$
    Find $(g.f)(3)$

Composition of Functions

Using $f(x) = x + 6$ and $g(x) = 3x$, find:

1) $f(g(1)) =$ ___
2) $f(g(-1)) =$ ___
3) $g(f(-3)) =$ ___
4) $g(f(4)) =$ ___
5) $f(g(2)) =$ ___
6) $g(f(3)) =$ ___

Using $f(x) = 2x + 5$ and $g(x) = x - 2$, find:

7) $g(f(2)) =$ ___
8) $g(f(-2)) =$ ___
9) $f(g(5)) =$ ___
10) $f(f(4)) =$ ___
11) $g(f(3)) =$ ___
12) $g(f(-3)) =$ ___

Using $f(x) = 4x - 2$ and $g(x) = x - 5$, find:

13) $g(f(-2)) =$ ___
14) $f(f(4)) =$ ___
15) $f(g(5)) =$ ___
16) $f(f(3)) =$ ___
17) $g(f(-3)) =$ ___
18) $g(g(6)) =$ ___

Using $f(x) = 6x + 2$ and $g(x) = 2x - 3$, find:

19) $f(g(-3)) =$ ___
20) $g(f(5)) =$ ___
21) $f(g(4)) =$ ___
22) $f(f(3)) =$ ___

Chapter 13: Functions Operations

Answers – Chapter 13

Function Notation and Evaluation

1) −5
2) 11
3) 10
4) −12
5) −9
6) −22
7) −15
8) −12
9) 5
10) −12
11) 25
12) 4
13) 22
14) 52
15) −1
16) 52
17) 70
18) −24
19) −505
20) −9x + 10
21) 4a + 5
22) 40x + 4

Adding and Subtracting Functions

1) −3
2) 0
3) −1
4) 10
5) −42
6) 4
7) −68
8) −122
9) $4a^2 − 9a − 11$
10) $−t^2 − 3t + 8$

Multiplying and Dividing Functions

1) 48
2) −42
3) 36
4) 8
5) 1
6) −9
7) −135
8) 140
9) $\frac{13}{122}$
10) −116

Chapter 13: Functions Operations

Composition of Functions

1) $f(g(1)) = 9$

2) $f(g(-1)) = 3$

3) $g(f(-3)) = 9$

4) $g(f(4)) = 30$

5) $f(g(2)) = 12$

6) $g(f(3)) = 27$

7) $g(f(2)) = 7$

8) $g(f(-2)) = -1$

9) $f(g(5)) = 11$

10) $f(f(4)) = 31$

11) $g(f(3)) = 9$

12) $g(f(-3)) = -3$

13) $g(f(-2)) = -15$

14) $f(f(4)) = 54$

15) $f(g(5)) = -2$

16) $f(f(3)) = 38$

17) $g(f(-3)) = -19$

18) $g(g(6)) = -4$

19) $f(g(-3)) = -52$

20) $g(f(5)) = 61$

21) $f(g(4)) = 32$

22) $f(f(3)) = 122$

Time to Tests

Time to refine your Math skill with a practice test

In this section, there are 2 complete Arithmetic Reasoning and Mathematics Knowledge ASVAB Tests. All practice tests are paper and pencil (P&P) ASVAB tests. Take these tests to see what score you'll be able to receive on a real ASVAB test. After you've finished, score your tests using the answer keys.

Before You Start

- You'll need a pencil and a timer to take the test.
- For each question, there are four possible answers. Choose which one is best.
- It's okay to guess. There is no penalty for wrong answers.
- Use the answer sheet provided to record your answers.
- After you've finished the test, review the answer key to see where you went wrong.

Calculators are NOT permitted for the ASVAB Test

Good luck

ASVAB Practice Test 1

2023

Section 1: Arithmetic Reasoning

30 questions

Total time for this section: 36 Minutes

You may NOT use a calculator on this section.

ASVAB Math Practice Test (Paper and Pencil) Answer Sheet

ASVAB Practice Test Arithmetic Reasoning

1	Ⓐ Ⓑ Ⓒ Ⓓ Ⓔ	11 Ⓐ Ⓑ Ⓒ Ⓓ Ⓔ	21 Ⓐ Ⓑ Ⓒ Ⓓ Ⓔ
2	Ⓐ Ⓑ Ⓒ Ⓓ Ⓔ	12 Ⓐ Ⓑ Ⓒ Ⓓ Ⓔ	22 Ⓐ Ⓑ Ⓒ Ⓓ Ⓔ
3	Ⓐ Ⓑ Ⓒ Ⓓ Ⓔ	13 Ⓐ Ⓑ Ⓒ Ⓓ Ⓔ	23 Ⓐ Ⓑ Ⓒ Ⓓ Ⓔ
4	Ⓐ Ⓑ Ⓒ Ⓓ Ⓔ	14 Ⓐ Ⓑ Ⓒ Ⓓ Ⓔ	24 Ⓐ Ⓑ Ⓒ Ⓓ Ⓔ
5	Ⓐ Ⓑ Ⓒ Ⓓ Ⓔ	15 Ⓐ Ⓑ Ⓒ Ⓓ Ⓔ	25 Ⓐ Ⓑ Ⓒ Ⓓ Ⓔ
6	Ⓐ Ⓑ Ⓒ Ⓓ Ⓔ	16 Ⓐ Ⓑ Ⓒ Ⓓ Ⓔ	26 Ⓐ Ⓑ Ⓒ Ⓓ Ⓔ
7	Ⓐ Ⓑ Ⓒ Ⓓ Ⓔ	17 Ⓐ Ⓑ Ⓒ Ⓓ Ⓔ	27 Ⓐ Ⓑ Ⓒ Ⓓ Ⓔ
8	Ⓐ Ⓑ Ⓒ Ⓓ Ⓔ	18 Ⓐ Ⓑ Ⓒ Ⓓ Ⓔ	28 Ⓐ Ⓑ Ⓒ Ⓓ Ⓔ
9	Ⓐ Ⓑ Ⓒ Ⓓ Ⓔ	19 Ⓐ Ⓑ Ⓒ Ⓓ Ⓔ	29 Ⓐ Ⓑ Ⓒ Ⓓ Ⓔ
10	Ⓐ Ⓑ Ⓒ Ⓓ Ⓔ	20 Ⓐ Ⓑ Ⓒ Ⓓ Ⓔ	30 Ⓐ Ⓑ Ⓒ Ⓓ Ⓔ

ASVAB Practice Test Mathematics Knowledge

1	Ⓐ Ⓑ Ⓒ Ⓓ Ⓔ	11 Ⓐ Ⓑ Ⓒ Ⓓ Ⓔ	21 Ⓐ Ⓑ Ⓒ Ⓓ Ⓔ
2	Ⓐ Ⓑ Ⓒ Ⓓ Ⓔ	12 Ⓐ Ⓑ Ⓒ Ⓓ Ⓔ	22 Ⓐ Ⓑ Ⓒ Ⓓ Ⓔ
3	Ⓐ Ⓑ Ⓒ Ⓓ Ⓔ	13 Ⓐ Ⓑ Ⓒ Ⓓ Ⓔ	23 Ⓐ Ⓑ Ⓒ Ⓓ Ⓔ
4	Ⓐ Ⓑ Ⓒ Ⓓ Ⓔ	14 Ⓐ Ⓑ Ⓒ Ⓓ Ⓔ	24 Ⓐ Ⓑ Ⓒ Ⓓ Ⓔ
5	Ⓐ Ⓑ Ⓒ Ⓓ Ⓔ	15 Ⓐ Ⓑ Ⓒ Ⓓ Ⓔ	25 Ⓐ Ⓑ Ⓒ Ⓓ Ⓔ
6	Ⓐ Ⓑ Ⓒ Ⓓ Ⓔ	16 Ⓐ Ⓑ Ⓒ Ⓓ Ⓔ	
7	Ⓐ Ⓑ Ⓒ Ⓓ Ⓔ	17 Ⓐ Ⓑ Ⓒ Ⓓ Ⓔ	
8	Ⓐ Ⓑ Ⓒ Ⓓ Ⓔ	18 Ⓐ Ⓑ Ⓒ Ⓓ Ⓔ	
9	Ⓐ Ⓑ Ⓒ Ⓓ Ⓔ	19 Ⓐ Ⓑ Ⓒ Ⓓ Ⓔ	
10	Ⓐ Ⓑ Ⓒ Ⓓ Ⓔ	20 Ⓐ Ⓑ Ⓒ Ⓓ Ⓔ	

1) Aria was hired to teach three identical math courses, which entailed being present in the classroom 36 hours altogether. At $25 per class hour, how much did Aria earn for teaching one course?

A. $50

B. $300

C. $600

D. $1,400

2) Karen is 9 years older than her sister Michelle, and Michelle is 4 years younger than her brother David. If the sum of their ages is 82, how old is Michelle?

A. 29

B. 27

C. 25

D. 23

3) John is driving to visit his mother, who lives 300 miles away. How long will the drive be, round-trip, if John drives at an average speed of 50 mph?

A. 95 *Minutes*

B. 260 *Minutes*

C. 645 *Minutes*

D. 720 *Minutes*

4) Julie gives 8 pieces of candy to each of her friends. If Julie gives all her candy away, which amount of candy could have been the amount she distributed?

A. 187

B. 216

C. 343

D. 223

5) There are only red and blue marbles in a box. The probability of choosing a red marble in the box at random is one fourth. If there are 132 blue marbles, how many marbles are in the box?

A. 140

B. 156

C. 176

D. 190

6) You are asked to chart the temperature during an 8-hour period to give the average. These are your results:

　　　　7 am: 2 degrees　　　　11 am: 32 degrees

　　　　8 am: 5 degrees　　　　12 pm: 35 degrees

　　　　9 am: 22 degrees　　　　1 pm: 35 degrees

　　　　10 am: 28 degrees　　　　2 pm: 33 degrees

What is the average temperature?

A. 36

B. 28

C. 24

D. 22

7) Each year, a cyber café charges its customers a base rate of $15, with an additional $0.20 per visit for the first 40 visits, and $0.10 for every visit after that. How much does the cyber café charge a customer for a year in which 60 visits are made?

A. $25

B. $29

C. $35

D. $39

8) If a vehicle is driven 32 miles on Monday, 35 miles on Tuesday, and 29 miles on Wednesday, what is the average number of miles driven each day?

A. 32 *Miles*

B. 31 *Miles*

C. 29 *Miles*

D. 27 *Miles*

9) Three co-workers contributed $10.25, $11.25, and $18.45 respectively to purchase a retirement gift for their boss. What is the maximum amount they can spend on a gift?

A. $42.25

B. $40.17

C. $39.95

D. $27.06

10) While at work, Emma checks her email once every 90 minutes. In 9-hour, how many times does she check her email?

A. 4 *Times*

B. 5 *Times*

C. 7 *Times*

D. 6 *Times*

11) A family owns 15 dozen of magazines. After donating 57 magazines to the public library, how many magazines are still with the family?

A. 180

B. 152

C. 123

D. 98

12) In the deck of cards, there are 4 spades, 3 hearts, 7 clubs, and 10 diamonds. What is the probability that William will pick out a spade?

A. $\frac{1}{5}$

B. $\frac{1}{6}$

C. $\frac{1}{8}$

D. $\frac{1}{9}$

13) What is the prime factorization of 560?

A. $2 \times 2 \times 5 \times 7$

B. $2 \times 2 \times 2 \times 2 \times 5 \times 7$

C. 2×7

D. $2 \times 2 \times 2 \times 5 \times 7$

14) William is driving a truck that can hold 5 tons maximum. He has a shipment of food weighing 32,000 pounds. How many trips will he need to make to deliver all of the food?

A. 1 *Trip*

B. 3 *Trips*

C. 4 *Trips*

D. 6 *Trips*

15) A man goes to a casino with $180. He loses $40 on blackjack, then loses another $50 on roulette. How much money does he have left?

A. $75

B. $90

C. $105

D. $120

16) A woman owns a dog walking business. If 3 workers can walk 9 dogs, how many dogs can 5 workers walk?

A. 13

B. 14

C. 15

D. 19

17) The mean of 50 test scores was calculated as 85. But, it turned out that one of the scores was misread as 94 but it was 69. What is the mean?

A. 84.5

B. 87

C. 87.5

D. 88.5

18) Mr. Carlos family are choosing a menu for their reception. They have 3 choices of appetizers, 7 choices of entrees, 4 choices of cake. How many different menu combinations are possible for them to choose?

A. 12

B. 32

C. 84

D. 120

19) The average of 6 numbers is 12. The average of 4 of those numbers is 10. What is the average of the other two numbers?

A. 10

B. 12

C. 14

D. 16

20) The average of five numbers is 24. If a sixth number 42 is added, then, what is the new average?

A. 25

B. 26

C. 27

D. 28

21) Jason needs an 76% average in his writing class to pass. On his first 4 exams, he earned scores of 68%, 72%, 85%, and 90%. What is the minimum score Jason can earn on his fifth and final test to pass?

A. 80%

B. 70%

C. 68%

D. 65%

22) 88 students took an exam and 11 of them failed. What percent of the students passed the exam?

A. 20%

B. 40.3%

C. 60%

D. 87.5%

23) Removing which of the following numbers will change the average of the numbers to 6?
1, 4, 5, 8, 11, 12

A. 1

B. 4

C. 5

D. 11

24) In two successive years, the population of a town is increased by 12% and 25%. What percent of the population is increased after two years?

A. 34%

B. 38%

C. 40%

D. 60%

25) Five years ago, Amy was three times as old as Mike was. If Mike is 10 years old now, how old is Amy?

A. 4

B. 8

C. 12

D. 20

26) If a tree casts a 18–foot shadow at the same time that a 4 feet yardstick casts a 3–foot shadow, what is the height of the tree?

A. 18 ft

B. 20 ft

C. 24 ft

D. 54 ft

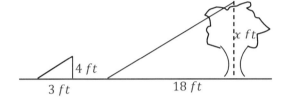

27) If a box contains red and blue balls in ratio of 2: 3, how many red balls are there if 90 blue balls are in the box?

A. 90

B. 60

C. 30

D. 10

28) If 30% of a number is 12, what is the number?

A. 12

B. 25

C. 40

D. 45

29) If $x \blacksquare y = \sqrt{x^2 + y}$, what is the value of $6 \blacksquare 28$?

A. $\sqrt{168}$

B. 10

C. 8

D. 6

30) The Edwards School is ordering some tables. If x is the number of tables the school wants to order, which each costs $100 and there is a one-time delivery charge of $800, which of the following represents the total cost, in dollar, per table?

A. $100x + 800$

B. $100 + 800x$

C. $\dfrac{100x+800}{100}$

D. $\dfrac{100x+800}{x}$

STOP: This is the End of Section 1 of test 1.

ASVAB Practice Test 1

2023

Section 2: Mathematics Knowledge

25 questions

Total time for this section: 24 Minutes

You may NOT use a calculator on this section.

1) If $a = 3$, what is the value of b in this equation?

$$b = \frac{a^2}{3} + 3$$

A. 10

B. 8

C. 6

D. 4

2) The eighth root of 256 is:

A. 6

B. 4

C. 8

D. 2

3) A circle has a radius of 5 inches. What is its approximate area? ($\pi = 3.14$)

A. 90.7 square inches

B. 78.5 square inches

C. 31.4 square inches

D. 25 square inches

4) If $-8a = 64$, then $a = $ ___

A. -8

B. 8

C. 16

D. 0

5) In the following diagram what is the value of x?

A. 90°

B. 60°

C. 45°

D. 15°

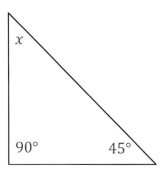

6) In the diagram below, circle A represents the set of all even numbers, circle B represents the set of all negative numbers, and circle C represents the set of all multiples of 6. Which number could be replaced with y?

A. 6

B. 0

C. −6

D. −10

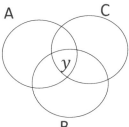

7) $(5x + 5)(2x + 6) = ?$

A. $5x + 6$

B. $10x^2 + 40x + 30$

C. $5x + 5x + 30$

D. $5x^2 + 5$

8) $5(a - 6) = 22$, what is the value of a?

A. 2.4

B. 10.4

C. 7

D. 11

9) If $3^{24} = 3^8 \times 3^x$, what is the value of x?

A. 2

B. 1.5

C. 3

D. 16

10) Which of the following is an obtuse angle?

A. 116°

B. 80°

C. 68°

D. 25°

11) Factor this expression: $x^2 + 5 - 6$

A. $x^2(5+6)$

B. $x(x+5-6)$

C. $(x+6)(x-1)$

D. $(x+6)(x-6)$

12) Find the slope of the line running through the points $(6, 7)$ and $(5, 3)$.

A. $\frac{1}{4}$

B. $\frac{1}{2}$

C. 4

D. 2

13) What is the value of $\sqrt{100} \times \sqrt{36}$?

A. 120

B. $\sqrt{136}$

C. 60

D. $\sqrt{16}$

14) Which of the following is not equal to 5^2?

A. the square of 5

B. 5 squared

C. 5 cubed

D. 5 to the second power

15) The cube root of 2,197 is?

A. 133

B. 13

C. 6.5

D. 169

16) What is 952,710 in scientific notation?

A. 95.271

B. 9.5271×10^5

C. 0.095271×10^6

D. 0.95271

17) What is the value of the expression $2(2x - y) + (4 - x)^2$ when $x = 2$ and $y = -1$?

A. -2

B. 8

C. 14

D. 28

18) A swimming pool holds 1,500 cubic feet of water. The swimming pool is 15 feet long and 10 feet wide. How deep is the swimming pool?

A. $2\ feet$

B. $4\ feet$

C. $6\ feet$

D. $10\ feet$

19) If $f(x) = x^3 - 2x^2 + 8x$ and $g(x) = 3$, what is the value of $f(g(x))$?

A. -3

B. 11

C. 22

D. 33

20) What is the solution of the following inequality?

$$|x - 2| \geq 4$$

A. $x \geq 6 \cup x \leq -2$

B. $-2 \leq x \leq 6$

C. $x \geq 6$

D. $x \leq -2$

21) Which of the following is equal to the expression below?
$$(3x - y)(2x + 2y)$$

A. $6x^2 - 2y^2$

B. $6x^2 + 4xy + 2y^2$

C. $12x^2 + 6xy + 2y^2$

D. $6x^2 + 4xy - 2y^2$

ASVAB Practice Test 1

22) What is the product of all possible values of x in the following equation?

$$|x - 12| = 4$$

A. 4

B. 8

C. 16

D. 128

23) In the triangle below, if the measure of angle A is 37 degrees, then what is the value of y? (figure is NOT drawn to scale)

A. 62

B. 70

C. 78

D. 86

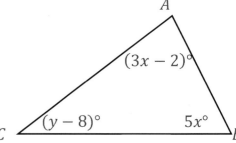

24) What is the perimeter of a square that has an area of 81 square inches?

A. $129\ inches$

B. $72\ inches$

C. $68\ inches$

D. $36\ inches$

25) What are the zeros of the function: $f(x) = x^2 - 7x + 12$?

A. 0

B. $-2, -3$

C. $0, 4, 3$

D. $4, 3$

STOP: This is the End of Section 2 of test 1.

ASVAB Practice Test 2

2023

Section 1: Arithmetic Reasoning

30 questions

Total time for this section: 36 Minutes

You may not use a calculator on this section.

ASVAB Math Practice Test (Paper and Pencil) Answer Sheet

ASVAB Practice Test Arithmetic Reasoning

1	Ⓐ Ⓑ Ⓒ Ⓓ Ⓔ	11	Ⓐ Ⓑ Ⓒ Ⓓ Ⓔ	21	Ⓐ Ⓑ Ⓒ Ⓓ Ⓔ
2	Ⓐ Ⓑ Ⓒ Ⓓ Ⓔ	12	Ⓐ Ⓑ Ⓒ Ⓓ Ⓔ	22	Ⓐ Ⓑ Ⓒ Ⓓ Ⓔ
3	Ⓐ Ⓑ Ⓒ Ⓓ Ⓔ	13	Ⓐ Ⓑ Ⓒ Ⓓ Ⓔ	23	Ⓐ Ⓑ Ⓒ Ⓓ Ⓔ
4	Ⓐ Ⓑ Ⓒ Ⓓ Ⓔ	14	Ⓐ Ⓑ Ⓒ Ⓓ Ⓔ	24	Ⓐ Ⓑ Ⓒ Ⓓ Ⓔ
5	Ⓐ Ⓑ Ⓒ Ⓓ Ⓔ	15	Ⓐ Ⓑ Ⓒ Ⓓ Ⓔ	25	Ⓐ Ⓑ Ⓒ Ⓓ Ⓔ
6	Ⓐ Ⓑ Ⓒ Ⓓ Ⓔ	16	Ⓐ Ⓑ Ⓒ Ⓓ Ⓔ	26	Ⓐ Ⓑ Ⓒ Ⓓ Ⓔ
7	Ⓐ Ⓑ Ⓒ Ⓓ Ⓔ	17	Ⓐ Ⓑ Ⓒ Ⓓ Ⓔ	27	Ⓐ Ⓑ Ⓒ Ⓓ Ⓔ
8	Ⓐ Ⓑ Ⓒ Ⓓ Ⓔ	18	Ⓐ Ⓑ Ⓒ Ⓓ Ⓔ	28	Ⓐ Ⓑ Ⓒ Ⓓ Ⓔ
9	Ⓐ Ⓑ Ⓒ Ⓓ Ⓔ	19	Ⓐ Ⓑ Ⓒ Ⓓ Ⓔ	29	Ⓐ Ⓑ Ⓒ Ⓓ Ⓔ
10	Ⓐ Ⓑ Ⓒ Ⓓ Ⓔ	20	Ⓐ Ⓑ Ⓒ Ⓓ Ⓔ	30	Ⓐ Ⓑ Ⓒ Ⓓ Ⓔ

ASVAB Practice Test Mathematics Knowledge

1	Ⓐ Ⓑ Ⓒ Ⓓ Ⓔ	11	Ⓐ Ⓑ Ⓒ Ⓓ Ⓔ	21	Ⓐ Ⓑ Ⓒ Ⓓ Ⓔ
2	Ⓐ Ⓑ Ⓒ Ⓓ Ⓔ	12	Ⓐ Ⓑ Ⓒ Ⓓ Ⓔ	22	Ⓐ Ⓑ Ⓒ Ⓓ Ⓔ
3	Ⓐ Ⓑ Ⓒ Ⓓ Ⓔ	13	Ⓐ Ⓑ Ⓒ Ⓓ Ⓔ	23	Ⓐ Ⓑ Ⓒ Ⓓ Ⓔ
4	Ⓐ Ⓑ Ⓒ Ⓓ Ⓔ	14	Ⓐ Ⓑ Ⓒ Ⓓ Ⓔ	24	Ⓐ Ⓑ Ⓒ Ⓓ Ⓔ
5	Ⓐ Ⓑ Ⓒ Ⓓ Ⓔ	15	Ⓐ Ⓑ Ⓒ Ⓓ Ⓔ	25	Ⓐ Ⓑ Ⓒ Ⓓ Ⓔ
6	Ⓐ Ⓑ Ⓒ Ⓓ Ⓔ	16	Ⓐ Ⓑ Ⓒ Ⓓ Ⓔ		
7	Ⓐ Ⓑ Ⓒ Ⓓ Ⓔ	17	Ⓐ Ⓑ Ⓒ Ⓓ Ⓔ		
8	Ⓐ Ⓑ Ⓒ Ⓓ Ⓔ	18	Ⓐ Ⓑ Ⓒ Ⓓ Ⓔ		
9	Ⓐ Ⓑ Ⓒ Ⓓ Ⓔ	19	Ⓐ Ⓑ Ⓒ Ⓓ Ⓔ		
10	Ⓐ Ⓑ Ⓒ Ⓓ Ⓔ	20	Ⓐ Ⓑ Ⓒ Ⓓ Ⓔ		

ASVAB Math Practice Workbook

1) Will has been working on a report for 6 hours each day, 7 days a week for 2 weeks. How many minutes has Will worked on his report?

A. 42

B. 84

C. 2,520

D. 5,040

2) James is driving to visit his mother, who lives 340 miles away. How long will the drive be, round-trip, if James drives at an average speed of 50 mph?

A. 135 $minutes$

B. 310 $minutes$

C. 741 $minutes$

D. 816 $minutes$

3) In a classroom of 60 students, 42 are female. What percentage of the class is male?

A. 36%

B. 34%

C. 30%

D. 26%

4) How many integers are between $\frac{7}{2}$ and $\frac{30}{4}$?

A. 3

B. 4

C. 6

D. 10

5) During the last week of track training, Emma achieves the following times in seconds: 66, 57, 54, 64, 57, and 59. Her three best times this week (least times) are averaged for her final score on the course. What is her final score?

A. 56 $seconds$

B. 57 $seconds$

C. 59 $seconds$

D. 61 $seconds$

6) How many square feet of tile is needed for a 15 feet × 15 feet room?

A. 225 $square\ feet$

B. 118.5 $square\ feet$

C. 112 $square\ feet$

D. 60 $square\ feet$

7) With what number must 1.303572 be multiplied in order to obtain the number 1303.572?

A. 100

B. 1,000

C. 10,000

D. 100,000

8) Which of the following is NOT a factor of 50?

A. 5

B. 2

C. 10

D. 15

9) Emma is working in a hospital supply room and makes $25.00 an hour. The union negotiates a new contract giving each employee a 4% cost of living raise. What is Emma's new hourly rate?

A. $26 *an hour*

B. $28 *an hour*

C. $30 *an hour*

D. $31.50 *an hour*

10) Emily and Lucas have taken the same number of photos on their school trip. Emily has taken 4 times as many photos as Mia. Lucas has taken 21 more photos than Mia. How many photos has Mia taken?

A. 7

B. 9

C. 11

D. 13

11) The set of possible values of n is $\{5, 3, 7\}$. What is the set of possible values of m if $2m = n + 5$?

A. $\{2, 4, 7\}$

B. $\{5, 4, 6\}$

C. $\{3, 2, 5\}$

D. $\{4, 5, 8\}$

12) Find the average of the following numbers: 22, 34, 16, 20

A. 23

B. 35

C. 30

D. 33

13) A mobile classroom is a rectangular block that is 90 feet by 30 feet in length and width respectively. If a student walks around the block once, how many yards does the student cover?

A. 2,700 $yards$

B. 240 $yards$

C. 120 $yards$

D. 60 $yards$

14) What is the distance in miles of a trip that takes 2.1 hours at an average speed of 16.2 miles per hour? (Round your answer to a whole number)

A. 44 $miles$

B. 34 $miles$

C. 30 $miles$

D. 18 $miles$

15) The sum of 6 numbers is greater than 120 and less than 180. Which of the following could be the average (arithmetic mean) of the numbers?

A. 20

B. 26

C. 30

D. 34

16) A barista averages making 15 coffees per hour. At this rate, how many hours will it take until she's made 1,500 coffees?

A. 95 $hours$

B. 90 $hours$

C. 100 $hours$

D. 105 $hours$

17) There are 120 rooms that need to be painted and only 12 painters available. If there are still 12 rooms unpainted by the end of the day, what is the average number of rooms that each painter has painted?

A. 9

B. 12

C. 14

D. 16

18) Nicole was making $7.50 per hour and got a raise to $7.8 per hour. What percentage increase was Nicole's raise?

A. 2%

B. 1.67%

C. 4%

D. 6.66%

19) An architect's floor plan uses ½ inch to represent one mile. What is the actual distance represented by 4 ½ inches?

A. 9 $miles$

B. 8 $miles$

C. 7 $miles$

D. 6 $miles$

20) A snack machine accepts only quarters. Candy bars cost 25¢, a package of peanuts costs 75¢, and a can of cola costs 50¢. How many quarters are needed to buy two Candy bars, one package of peanuts, and one can of cola?

A. 8 $quarters$

B. 7 $quarters$

C. 6 $quarters$

D. 5 $quarters$

21) The hour hand of a watch rotates 30 degrees every hour. How many complete rotations does the hour hand make in 8 days?

A. 12

B. 14

C. 16

D. 18

22) What is the product of the square root of 81 and the square root of 25?

A. 2,025

B. 15

C. 25

D. 45

23) If $2y + 4y + 2y = -24$, then what is the value of y?

A. -3

B. -2

C. -1

D. 0

24) A bread recipe calls for $2\frac{2}{3}$ cups of flour. If you only have $1\frac{5}{6}$ cups of flour, how much more flour is needed?

A. 1

B. $\frac{1}{2}$

C. 2

D. $\frac{5}{6}$

25) Convert 0.023 to a percent.

A. 0.2%

B. 0.23%

C. 2.30%

D. 23%

26) If $0.00104 = \frac{104}{x}$, what is the value of x?

A. 1,000

B. 10,000

C. 100,000

D. 1,000,000

27) A writer finishes 180 pages of his manuscript in 20 hours. How many pages is his average per hour?

A. 18

B. 6

C. 3

D. 9

28) Camille uses a 30% off coupon when buying a sweater that costs $50. If she also pays 5% sales tax on the purchase, how much does she pay?

A. $35

B. $36.75

C. $39.95

D. $47.17

29) I've got 34 quarts of milk and my family drinks 2 gallons of milk per week. How many weeks will that last us?

A. 2 *weeks*

B. 2.5 *weeks*

C. 3.25 *weeks*

D. 4.25 *weeks*

30) A floppy disk shows 937,036 bytes free and 739,352 bytes used. If you delete a file of size 652,159 bytes and create a new file of size 599,986 bytes, how many free bytes will the floppy disk have?

A. 687,179

B. 791,525

C. 884,867

D. 989,209

STOP: This is the End of Section 1 of test 2.

ASVAB Practice Test 2

2023

Section 2: Mathematics Knowledge

25 questions

Total time for this section: 24 Minutes

You may NOT use a calculator on this section.

ASVAB Practice Test 2

1) $(x+7)(x+5) = ?$
A. $x^2 + 12x + 12$
B. $x^2 + 12x + 12$
C. $x^2 + 35x + 12$
D. $x^2 + 12x + 35$

2) Convert 670,000 to scientific notation.
A. $6.70 \times 1,000$
B. 6.70×10^{-5}
C. 6.70×100
D. 6.7×10^5

3) What is the perimeter of the triangle in the provided diagram?
A. 15,625
B. 625
C. 75
D. 25

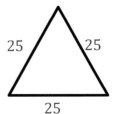

4) If x is a positive integer divisible by 6, and $x < 60$, what is the greatest possible value of x?
A. 54
B. 48
C. 36
D. 59

5) There are two pizza ovens in a restaurant. Oven 1 burns four times as many pizzas as oven 2. If the restaurant had a total of 15 burnt pizzas on Saturday, how many pizzas did oven 2 burn?
A. 3
B. 6
C. 9
D. 12

6) What is the value of x in the figure below?
A. 32°
B. 46°
C. 54°
D. 63°

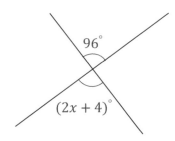

7) If $8 + 2x$ is 16 more than 20, what is the value of $6x$?

A. 40

B. 55

C. 62

D. 84

8) If a gas tank can hold 30 gallons, how many gallons does it contain when it is $\frac{3}{5}$ full?

A. 27

B. 24

C. 21

D. 18

9) In the xy-plane, the point $(4, 3)$ and $(3, 2)$ are on line A. Which of the following equations of lines is parallel to line A?

A. $y = 3x$

B. $y = \frac{x}{2}$

C. $y = 2x$

D. $y = x$

10) A circle has a diameter of 16 inches. What is its approximate area? ($\pi = 3.14$)

A. 200.96

B. 100.48

C. 64.00

D. 12.56

11) If $y = (-3x^3)^2$, which of the following expressions is equal to y?

A. $-6x^5$

B. $-6x^6$

C. $6x^5$

D. $9x^6$

12) The equation of a line is given as: $y = 5x - 3$. Which of the following points does not lie on the line?

A. $(1, 2)$

B. $(-2, -13)$

C. $(3, 18)$

D. $(2, 7)$

13) When $P + Q = 12$ and $3R + Q = 12$, what is the value of R?

A. 12

B. 2

C. 0

D. It cannot be determined from the information given.

14) What is the distance between the points $(1, 3)$ and $(-2, 7)$?

A. 3

B. 4

C. 5

D. 6

15) $x^2 - 81 = 0$, x could be:

A. 6

B. 9

C. 12

D. 15

16) A rectangular plot of land is measured to be 160 feet by 200 feet. Its total area is:

A. 32,000 square feet

B. 4,404 square feet

C. 3,200 square feet

D. 2,040 square feet

17) In the figure below, line A is parallel to line B. What is the value of angle x?

A. 45 degree

B. 55 degree

C. 80 degree

D. 120 degree

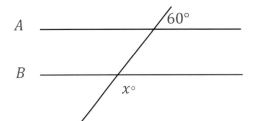

18) What is the length of AB in the following figure if $AE = 6$, $CD = 9$ and $AC = 24$?

A. 6.8

B. 8.2

C. 9.6

D. 18

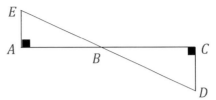

19) John buys a pepper plant that is 6 inches tall. With regular watering the plant grows 4 inches a year. Writing John's plant's height as a function of time, what does the $y-$intercept represent?

A. The $y-$intercept represents the rate of grows of the plant which is 5 inches

B. The $y-$intercept represents the starting height of 6 inches

C. The $y-$intercept represents the rate of growth of plant which is 3 inches per year

D. There is no $y-$intercept

20) One fourth the cube of 4 is:

A. 32

B. 25

C. 16

D. 8

21) What is the sum of the prime numbers in the following list of numbers?

$$14, 12, 11, 16, 13, 20, 19, 36, 30$$

A. 43

B. 37

C. 32

D. 26

22) If $f(x^2) = 3x + 5$, for all positive value of x, what is the value of $f(144)$?

A. 367

B. 41

C. 29

D. −29

23) The supplement angle of a 45° angle is:

A. 135°

B. 105°

C. 90°

D. 35°

24) Which of the following is the solution of the following inequality?
$$3.5x - 17.5 < 2x - 5 - 3.5x$$

A. $x < 2.5$

B. $x > -4.11$

C. $x \leq 3$

D. $x \geq -3$

25) Simplify: $5(2x^6)^3$.

A. $10x^9$

B. $10x^{18}$

C. $40x^{18}$

D. $40x^9$

STOP: This is the End of Section 2 of test 2.

ASVAB Math Practice Tests Answer Keys

Now, it's time to review your results to see where you went wrong and what areas you need to improve.

ASVAB Math Practice Test 1					
Arithmetic Reasoning			**Mathematics Knowledge**		
1)	B	16)	C	1)	C	16)	B
2)	D	17)	A	2)	D	17)	C
3)	D	18)	C	3)	B	18)	D
4)	B	19)	D	4)	A	19)	D
5)	C	20)	C	5)	C	20)	A
6)	C	21)	D	6)	C	21)	D
7)	A	22)	D	7)	B	22)	D
8)	A	23)	D	8)	B	23)	D
9)	C	24)	C	9)	D	24)	D
10)	D	25)	D	10)	A	25)	D
11)	C	26)	C	11)	C
12)	B	27)	B	12)	C
13)	B	28)	C	13)	C
14)	C	29)	C	14)	C
15)	B	30)	D	15)	B

ASVAB Math Practice Test 2

Arithmetic Reasoning				Mathematics Knowledge			
1)	D	16)	C	1)	D	16)	A
2)	D	17)	A	2)	D	17)	D
3)	C	18)	C	3)	C	18)	C
4)	B	19)	A	4)	A	19)	B
5)	A	20)	B	5)	A	20)	C
6)	A	21)	C	6)	B	21)	A
7)	B	22)	D	7)	D	22)	B
8)	D	23)	A	8)	D	23)	A
9)	A	24)	D	9)	D	24)	A
10)	A	25)	C	10)	A	25)	C
11)	B	26)	C	11)	D		
12)	A	27)	D	12)	C		
13)	B	28)	B	13)	D		
14)	B	29)	D	14)	C		
15)	B	30)	D	15)	B		

ASVAB Practice Tests Answers and Explanations

ASVAB Practice Test 1: Arithmetic Reasoning

1) Choice B is correct

$36 \div 3 = 12$ hours for one course, $12 \times 25 = 300 \Rightarrow \$300$

2) Choice D is correct

Karen = Michelle +9, Michelle = David −4, Karen + Michelle + David = 82

Michelle = David −4 ⇒ David = Michelle + 4

Now, replace the ages of Karen and David by Michelle. Then:

Michelle +9 + Michelle + Michelle +4 = 82, 3Michelle +13 = 82 ⇒ 3Michelle = 82 − 13

3Michelle = 69, Michelle = 23

3) Choice D is correct

$distance = speed \times time \Rightarrow time = \frac{distance}{speed} = \frac{600}{50} = 12$

(Round trip means that the distance is 600 miles)

The round trip takes 12 hours. Change hours to minutes, then: $12 \times 60 = 720$

4) Choice B is correct

Since Julie gives 8 pieces of candy to each of her friends, then, then number of pieces of candies must be divisible by 8.

A. $187 \div 8 = 23.375$
B. $216 \div 8 = 27$
C. $343 \div 8 = 42.875$
D. $223 \div 8 = 27.875$

Only choice B gives a whole number.

5) Choice C is correct

let x be total number of marbles in the box, then number of red marbles is: $x - 132$

$p = \frac{1}{4} = \frac{x-132}{x}$, Use cross multiplication to solve for x.

$x = 4(x - 132) \to x = 4x - 528 \to 3x = 528 \to x = 176$

6) Choice C is correct

$average = \frac{sum}{total}$, Sum $= 2 + 5 + 22 + 28 + 32 + 35 + 35 + 33 = 192$

Total number of results = 8, $average = \frac{192}{8} = 24$

7) Choice A is correct

The base rate is \$15. The fee for the first 40 visits is: $40 \times 0.20 = 8$

The fee for the visits 41 to 60 is: $20 \times 0.10 = 2$,   Total charge: $15 + 8 + 2 = 25$

8) Choice A is correct

$average = \frac{sum}{total} = \frac{32+35+29}{3} = \frac{96}{3} = 32$

9) Choice C is correct

The amount they have = \$10.25 + \$11.25 + \$18.45 = 39.95

10) Choice D is correct

Change 9 hours to minutes, then: $9 \times 60 = 540$ minutes, $\frac{540}{90} = 6$

11) Choice C is correct

15 dozen of magazines are 180 magazines: $15 \times 12 = 180$, $180 - 57 = 123$

12) Choice B is correct

$probability = \frac{desired\ outcomes}{possible\ outcomes} = \frac{4}{4+3+7+10} = \frac{4}{24} = \frac{1}{6}$

13) Choice B is correct

Find the value of each choice:

A. $2 \times 2 \times 5 \times 7 = 140$

B. $2 \times 2 \times 2 \times 2 \times 5 \times 7 = 560$

C. $2 \times 7 = 14$

D. $2 \times 2 \times 2 \times 5 \times 7 = 280$

14) Choice C is correct

$1\ ton = 2,000\ pounds, 5\ ton = 10,000\ pounds$, $\frac{32,000}{10,000} = 3.2$

William needs to make at least 4 trips to deliver all of the food.

15) Choice B is correct

$180 - 40 - 50 = 90$

ASVAB Math Practice Workbook

16) Choice C is correct

Each worker can walk 3 dogs: $9 \div 3 = 3$, 5 workers can walk 15 dogs. $5 \times 3 = 15$

17) Choice A is correct

$average\ (mean) = \frac{sum\ of\ terms}{number\ of\ terms} \Rightarrow 85 = \frac{sum\ of\ terms}{50} \Rightarrow sum = 85 \times 50 = 4,250$

The difference of 94 and 69 is 25. Therefore, 25 should be subtracted from the sum.

$4,250 - 25 = 4,225, mean = \frac{sum\ of\ terms}{number\ of\ terms} \Rightarrow mean = \frac{4,225}{50} = 84.5$

18) Choice C is correct

To find the number of possible outfit combinations, multiply number of options for each factor:

$3 \times 7 \times 4 = 84$

19) Choice D is correct

$average = \frac{sum\ of\ terms}{number\ of\ terms} \Rightarrow$

(average of 6 numbers) $12 = \frac{sum\ of\ numbers}{6} \Rightarrow$ sum of 6 numbers is $12 \times 6 = 72$

(average of 4 numbers) $10 = \frac{sum\ of\ numbers}{4} \Rightarrow$ sum of 4 numbers is $10 \times 4 = 40$

$sum\ of\ 6\ number - sum\ of\ 4\ numbers = sum\ of\ 2\ numbers$

$72 - 40 = 32$, average of 2 numbers $= \frac{32}{2} = 16$

20) Choice C is correct

Solve for the sum of five numbers.

$average = \frac{sum\ of\ terms}{number\ of\ terms} \Rightarrow 24 = \frac{sum\ of\ 5\ numbers}{5} \Rightarrow sum\ of\ 5\ numbers = 24 \times 5 = 120$

The sum of 5 numbers is 120. If a sixth number 42 is added, then the sum of 6 numbers is

$120 + 42 = 162, average = \frac{sum\ of\ terms}{number\ of\ terms} = \frac{162}{6} = 27$

21) Choice D is correct

Jason needs an 76% average to pass for five exams. Therefore, the sum of 5 exams must be at lease $5 \times 76 = 380$, The sum of 4 exams is: $68 + 72 + 85 + 90 = 315$.

The minimum score Jason can earn on his fifth and final test to pass is: $380 - 315 = 65$

ASVAB Practice Tests Answers and Explanations

22) Choice D is correct

The failing rate is 11 out of 88 = $\frac{11}{88}$, Change the fraction to percent: $\frac{11}{88} \times 100\% = 12.5\%$

12.5 percent of students failed. Therefore, 87.5 percent of students passed the exam.

23) Choice D is correct

Check each choice provided:

A. 1 $\frac{4+5+8+11+12}{5} = \frac{40}{5} = 8$

B. 4 $\frac{1+5+8+11+12}{5} = \frac{37}{5} = 7.4$

C. 5 $\frac{1+4+8+11+12}{5} = \frac{36}{5} = 7.2$

D. 11 $\frac{1+4+5+8+12}{5} = \frac{30}{5} = 6$

24) Choice C is correct

The population is increased by 12% and 25%. 12% increase changes the population to 112% of original population. For the second increase, multiply the result by 125%:

$(1.12) \times (1.25) = 1.40 = 140\%$, 40 percent of the population is increased after two years.

25) Choice D is correct

Five years ago, Amy was three times as old as Mike. Mike is 10 years now. Therefore, 5 years ago Mike was 5 years. Five years ago, Amy was: $A = 3 \times 5 = 15$, Now Amy is 20 years old:

$15 + 5 = 20$

26) Choice C is correct

Write a proportion and solve for x: $\frac{4}{3} = \frac{x}{18} \Rightarrow 3x = 18 \times 4 \Rightarrow x = \frac{72}{3} = 24\ ft$

27) Choice B is correct

$\frac{2}{3} \times 90 = 60$

28) Choice C is correct

Let x be the number. Write the equation and solve for x.

$30\%\ of\ x = 12 \Rightarrow 0.30x = 12 \Rightarrow x = 12 \div 0.30 = 40$

29) Choice C is correct

Substitute x by 6 and y by 28 in the equation. Then:

$6 \blacksquare 28 = \sqrt{6^2 + 28} = \sqrt{36 + 28} = \sqrt{64} = 8$

30) Choice D is correct

The amount of money for x tables is: $100x$, then, the total cost of all tables is equal to:

$100x + 800$, the total cost, in dollar, per table is: $\frac{Total\ cost}{number\ of\ tables} = \frac{100x + 800}{x}$

ASVAB Practice Test 1: Mathematics Knowledge

1) **Choice C is correct**

If $a = 3$ then: $b = \frac{a^2}{3} + 3 \rightarrow b = \frac{3^2}{3} + 3 = 3 + 3 = 6$

2) **Choice D is correct**

$\sqrt[8]{256} = 2$ ($2^8 = 2 \times 2 \times 2 \times 2 \times 2 \times 2 \times 2 \times 2 = 256$)

3) **Choice B is correct**

($r = radius$)

Area of a circle $= \pi r^2 = \pi \times (5)^2 = 3.14 \times 25 = 78.5$

4) **Choice A is correct**

$-8a = 64 \rightarrow a = \frac{64}{-8} = -8$

5) **Choice C is correct**

All angles in a triable add up to 180 degrees. $90° + 45° = 135°$, $x = 180° - 135° = 45°$

6) **Choice C is correct**

y is the intersection of the three circles. Therefore, it must be even (from circle A), negative (from circle B), and multiple of 6 (from circle C). From the choice, only -6 is even, negative and multiple of 6.

7) **Choice B is correct**

Use FOIL (first, out, in, last) method.

$(5x + 5)(2x + 6) = 10x^2 + 30x + 10x + 30 = 10x^2 + 40x + 30$

8) **Choice B is correct**

$5(a - 6) = 22 \Rightarrow 5a - 30 = 22 \Rightarrow 5a = 22 + 30 \Rightarrow 5a = 52 \Rightarrow 5a = 52 \Rightarrow a = \frac{52}{5} = 10.4$

9) **Choice D is correct**

Use exponent multiplication rule: $x^a \cdot x^b = x^{a+b}$ Then: $3^{24} = 3^8 \times 3^x = 3^{8+x}$

$24 = 8 + x \Rightarrow x = 24 - 8 = 16$

10) **Choice A is correct**

An obtuse angle is an angle of greater than 90 degrees and less than 180 degrees. Only choice A is an obtuse angle.

11) Choice C is correct

To factor the expression $x^2 + 5 - 6$, we need to find two numbers whose sum is 5 and their product is -6. Those numbers are 6 and -1. Then: $x^2 + 5 - 6 = (x + 6)(x - 1)$

12) Choice C is correct

Slope of a line: $\frac{y_2 - y_1}{x_2 - x_1} = \frac{rise}{run}$

$\frac{y_2 - y_1}{x_2 - x_1} = \frac{3 - 7}{5 - 6} = \frac{-4}{-1} = 4$

13) Choice C is correct

$\sqrt{100} = 10, \quad \sqrt{36} = 6, \quad 10 \times 6 = 60$

14) Choice C is correct

Only choice C is not equal to 5^2.

15) Choice B is correct

$\sqrt[3]{2,197} = 13$

16) Choice B is correct

In scientific notation form, numbers are written with one whole number times 10 to the power of a whole number. Number 952,710 has 6 digits. Write the number and after the first digit put the decimal point. Then, multiply the number by 10 to the power of 5 (number of remaining digits). Then: $952,710 = 9.5271 \times 10^5$

17) Choice C is correct

Plug in the value of x and y: $x = 2$ and $y = -1$

$2(2x - y) + (4 - x)^2 = x^2 - 4x - 2y + 16 = (2)^2 - 4(2) - 2(-1) + 16 = 14$

18) Choice D is correct

Use formula of rectangle prism volume: $V = (length)(width)(height) \Rightarrow$

$1,500 = (15)(10)(height) \Rightarrow height = 1,500 \div 150 = 10$

19) Choice D is correct

$g(x) = 3$, then $f(g(x)) = f(3) = (3)^3 - 2(3)^2 + 8(3) = 27 - 18 + 24 = 33$

ASVAB Practice Tests Answers and Explanations

20) Choice A is correct

$|x - 2| \geq 4$. Then: $x - 2 \geq 4$ or $x - 2 \leq 4$. Solve both inequalities: $x - 2 \geq 4 \rightarrow x \geq 6$ and $x - 2 \leq 4 \rightarrow x \leq 6$. The solution of the inequality $|x - 2| \geq 4$ is $x \geq 6 \cup x \leq -2$

21) Choice D is correct

Use FOIL method: $(3x - y)(2x + 2y) = 6x^2 + 6xy - 2xy - 2y^2 = 6x^2 + 4xy - 2y^2$

22) Choice D is correct

To solve absolute values equations, write two equations. $x - 12$ could be positive 4, or negative -4. Therefore, $x - 12 = 4 \Rightarrow x = 16$, $x - 12 = -4 \Rightarrow x = 8$. Find the product of solutions: $8 \times 16 = 128$

23) Choice D is correct

In the figure angle A is labeled $(3x - 2)$ and it measures 37. Thus, $3x - 2 = 37$ and $3x = 39$ or $x = 13$. That means that angle B, which is labeled $(5x)$, must measure $5 \times 13 = 65$.

Since the three angles of a triangle must add up to 180, $37 + 65 + y - 8 = 180$, then:

$y + 94 = 180 \rightarrow y = 180 - 94 = 86$

24) Choice D is correct

The area of the square is 81 inches. Therefore, the side of the square is square root of the area. $\sqrt{81} = 9$ inches. Four times the side of the square is the perimeter: $4 \times 9 = 36 \ inches$

25) Choice D is correct

First factor the function: $(x - 4)(x - 3)$. To find the zeros, f(x) should be zero:

$f(x) = (x - 4)(x - 3) = 0$, Therefore, the zeros are, $(x - 4) = 0 \Rightarrow x = 4$, $(x - 3) = 0 \Rightarrow x = 3$

ASVAB Practice Test 2: Arithmetic Reasoning

1) **Choice D is correct**

2 weeks = 14 days,   Then: 14 × 6 = 84 hours,   84 × 60 = 5,040 minutes

2) **Choice D is correct**

$distance = speed \times time \Rightarrow time = \frac{distance}{speed} = \frac{340+340}{50} = 13.6$

(Round trip means that the distance is 680 miles)

The round trip takes 13.6 hours. Change hours to minutes, then: $13.6 \times 60 = 816$

3) **Choice C is correct**

$60 - 42 = 18$ male students. $\frac{18}{60} = 0.3$,   Change 0.3 to percent $\Rightarrow 0.3 \times 100 = 30\%$

4) **Choice B is correct**

First, change the improper fractions into mixed numbers: $\frac{7}{2} = 3\frac{1}{2}$ and $\frac{30}{4} = 7\frac{1}{2}$

The integers between these two values are 4, 5, 6 and 7. So, there are 4 integers between $\frac{7}{5}$ and $\frac{30}{4}$.

5) **Choice A is correct**

Emma's three best times are 54, 57, and 57. The average of these numbers is: $average = \frac{sum}{total}$

$Sum = 54 + 57 + 57 = 168$. Total number of numbers = 3 $average = \frac{168}{3} = 56$

6) **Choice A is correct**

The area of a 15 feet × 15 feet room is 225 square feet. $15 \times 15 = 225$

7) **Choice B is correct**

$1.303572 \times 1,000 = 1303.572$

8) **Choice D is correct**

The factors of 50 are: {1, 2, 5, 10, 25, 50}. 15 is not a factor of 50.

9) **Choice A is correct**

4 percent of 25 is: $25 \times \frac{4}{100} = 1$,   Emma's new rate is 26. $25 + 1 = 26$

ASVAB Practice Tests Answers and Explanations

10) Choice A is correct

Emily = Lucas, Emily = 4 Mia ⇒ Lucas = 4 Mia, Lucas = Mia + 21, then:

Lucas = Mia + 21 ⇒ 4 Mia = Mia + 21.

Remove 1 Mia from both sides of the equation. Then: 3 Mia = 21 ⇒ Mia = 7

11) Choice B is correct

$2m = n + 5 \to m = \frac{n+5}{2}$. Substitute each value of n to find the values of m:

$m = \frac{5+5}{2} = \frac{10}{2} = 5$

$m = \frac{3+5}{2} = \frac{8}{2} = 4$

$m = \frac{7+5}{2} = \frac{12}{2} = 6$

The set of m is {5,4,6}

12) Choice A is correct

$Sum = 22 + 34 + 16 + 20 = 92, \quad average = \frac{92}{4} = 23$

13) Choice B is correct

$Perimeter\ of\ a\ rectangle = 2 \times length + 2 \times width =$

$2 \times 90 + 2 \times 30 = 180 + 60 = 240$

14) Choice B is correct

$Speed = \frac{distance}{time}, \quad 16.2 = \frac{distance}{2.1} \Rightarrow distance = 16.2 \times 2.1 = 34.02$

Rounded to a whole number, the answer is 34.

15) Choice B is correct

Let's review the choices provided and find their sum.

A. $20 \times 6 = 120$
B. $26 \times 6 = 144 \Rightarrow$ is greater than 120 and less than 180
C. $30 \times 6 = 180$
D. $34 \times 6 = 204$

Only choice B gives a number that is greater than 120 and less than 180.

16) Choice C is correct

$\frac{1\ hour}{15\ coffees} = \frac{x}{1,500} \Rightarrow 15 \times x = 1 \times 1,500 \Rightarrow 15x = 1,500 \Rightarrow x = 100$

It takes 100 hours until she's made 1,500 coffees.

17) Choice A is correct

$120 - 12 = 108$, $\frac{108}{12} = 9$

18) Choice C is correct

$Percent\ of\ Change = \frac{New\ Value - Old\ Value}{Old\ Value} \times 100\% = \frac{7.80 - 7.50}{7.50} \times 100\% = 4\%$

19) Choice A is correct

Write a proportion and solve. $\frac{\frac{1}{2} inches}{4.5} = \frac{1\ mile}{x}$

Use cross multiplication, then: $\frac{1}{2}x = 4.5 \rightarrow x = 9$

20) Choice B is correct

Two candy bars costs 50¢ and a package of peanuts cost 75¢ and a can of cola costs 50¢. The total cost is: $50 + 75 + 50 = 175$, 175 is equal to 7 quarters. $7 \times 25 = 175$

21) Choice C is correct

Every day the hour hand of a watch makes 2 complete rotation. Thus, it makes 16 complete rotations in 8 days. $2 \times 8 = 16$

22) Choice D is correct

$\sqrt{81} \times \sqrt{25} = 9 \times 5 = 45$

23) Choice A is correct

$2y + 4y + 2y = -24 \Rightarrow 8y = -24 \Rightarrow y = -\frac{24}{8} \Rightarrow y = -3$

24) Choice D is correct

$2\frac{2}{3} - 1\frac{5}{6} = 2\frac{4}{6} - 1\frac{5}{6} = \frac{16}{6} - \frac{11}{6} = \frac{5}{6}$

25) Choice C is correct

To convert a decimal to percent, multiply it by 100 and then add percent sign (%). $0.023 \times 100 = 2.30\%$

26) Choice C is correct

Solve for x: $0.00104 = \frac{104}{x}$, multiply both sides by x, $(0.00104)(x) = \frac{104}{x}(x)$.

ASVAB Practice Tests Answers and Explanations

Simplify: $0.00104x = 104$. Divide both side by 0.00104: $\frac{0.00104x}{0.00104} = \frac{104}{0.00104}$, simplify

$x = \frac{104}{0.00104} = 100,000$

27) Choice D is correct

$180 \div 20 = 9$

28) Choice B is correct

$30\% \times 50 = \frac{30}{100} \times 50 = 15$, The coupon has $15 value. Then, the selling price of the sweater is $35. $50 - 15 = 35$ Add 5% tax, then: $\frac{5}{100} \times 35 = 1.75$ for tax. then: $35 + 1.75 = \$36.75$

29) Choice D is correct

1 quart = 0.25 gallon, 34 quarts = $34 \times 0.25 = 8.5$ gallons, then: $\frac{8.5}{2} = 4.25$ weeks

30) Choice D is correct

The difference of the file added, and the file deleted is: $652,159 - 599,986 = 52,173$

$937,036 + 52,173 = 989,209$

ASVAB Practice Test 2: Mathematics Knowledge

1) **Choice D is correct**

Use FOIL (First, Out, In, Last) method.

$(x+7)(x+5) = x^2 + 5x + 7x + 35 = x^2 + 12x + 35$

2) **Choice D is correct**

In scientific notation form, numbers are written with one whole number times 10 to the power of a whole number. Number 670,000 has 6 digits. Write the number and after the first digit put the decimal point. Then, multiply the number by 10 to the power of 5 (number of remaining digits). Then: $670,000 = 6.7 \times 10^5$

3) **Choice C is correct**

$Perimeter\ of\ a\ triangle = side\ 1 + side\ 2 + side\ 3 = 25 + 25 + 25 = 75$

4) **Choice A is correct**

From the choices provided, 36, 48 and 54 are divisible by 6. From these numbers, 54 is the biggest.

5) **Choice A is correct**

Oven 1 = 4 oven 2. If Oven 2 burns 3 then oven 1 burns 12 pizzas. $3 + 12 = 15$

6) **Choice B is correct**

$(2x + 4)°$ and $96°$ are vertical angles. Vertical angles are equal in measure. Then:

$2x + 4 = 96 \rightarrow 2x = 92 \rightarrow x = 46°$

7) **Choice D is correct**

The description $8 + 2x\ is\ 16$ more than 20 can be written as the equation $8 + 2x = 16 + 20$, which is equivalent to $8 + 2x = 36$. Subtracting 8 from each side of $8 + 2x = 36$ gives $2x = 28$. Since $6x$ is 3 times $2x$, multiplying both sides of $2x = 28$ by 3 gives $6x = 84$.

8) **Choice D is correct**

$\frac{3}{5} \times 30 = \frac{90}{5} = 18$

9) **Choice D is correct**

The slop of line A is: $m = \frac{y_2 - y_1}{x_2 - x_1} = \frac{3-2}{4-3} = 1$, Parallel lines have the same slope and only choice D ($y = x$) has slope of 1.

ASVAB Practice Tests Answers and Explanations

10) Choice A is correct

Diameter = 16, then: Radius = 8, Area of a circle = $\pi r^2 \Rightarrow A = 3.14(8)^2 = 200.96$

11) Choice D is correct

$y = (-3x^3)^2 = (-3)^2(x^3)^2 = 9x^6$

12) Choice C is correct

Let's review the choices provided. Put the values of x and y in the equation.

A. $(1, 2)$ $\Rightarrow x = 1 \Rightarrow y = 2$ This is true.

B. $(-2, -13)$ $\Rightarrow x = -2 \Rightarrow y = -13$ This is true.

C. $(3, 18)$ $\Rightarrow x = 3 \Rightarrow y = 12$ This is not true.

D. $(2, 7)$ $\Rightarrow x = 2 \Rightarrow y = 7$ This is true.

13) Choice D is correct

In the question, there are two equations and three variables. Therefore, it cannot be determined from the information given.

14) Choice C is correct

Use distance formula:

$d = \sqrt{(x_1 - x_2)^2 + (y_1 - y_2)^2} = \sqrt{(1-(-2))^2 + (3-7)^2} = \sqrt{9+16} = \sqrt{25} = 5$

15) Choice B is correct

$x^2 - 81 = 0 \Rightarrow x^2 = 81$ x could be 9 or -9.

16) Choice A is correct

$Area\ of\ a\ rectangle = width \times length = 160 \times 200 = 32,000$

17) Choice D is correct

The angle x and 60 are complementary angles. Therefore: $x + 60 = 180, 180° - 60° = 120°$

18) Choice C is correct

Two triangles ΔBAE and ΔBCD are similar. Then:

$\frac{AE}{CD} = \frac{AB}{BC} = \frac{6}{9}$ and $AC = 24$. Let's put x for AB. Then: $AC = AB + BC = x + (24 - x)$.

$\frac{6}{9} = \frac{x}{24-x} \rightarrow 144 - 6x = 9x \rightarrow 15x = 144 \rightarrow x = 9.6$

19) Choice B is correct

To solve this problem, first recall the equation of a line: $y = mx + b$

Where, $m = slope$ and $y = y - intercept$, Remember that slope is the rate of change that occurs in a function and that the y −intercept is the y value corresponding to $x = 0$.

Since the height of John's plant is 6 inches tall when he gets it. Time (or x) is zero. The plant grows 4 inches per year. Therefore, the rate of change of the plant's height is 4. The y −intercept represents the starting height of the plant which is 6 inches.

20) Choice C is correct

The cube of $4 = 4 \times 4 \times 4 = 64 \quad \frac{1}{4} \times 64 = 16$

21) Choice A is correct

From the list of numbers, 11, 13, and 19 are prime numbers. Their sum is:

$11 + 13 + 19 = 43$

22) Choice B is correct

$x^2 = 144 \rightarrow x = 12$ (positive value) $\qquad$ Or $\qquad x = -12$ (negative value)

Since x is positive, then: $f(144) = f(12^2) = 3(12) + 5 = 36 + 5 = 41$

23) Choice A is correct

Two Angles are supplementary when they add up to 180 degrees.

$135° + 45° = 180°$

24) Choice A is correct

$3.5x - 17.5 < 2x - 5 - 3.5x \rightarrow$ Combine like terms: $3.5x - 17.5 < -1.5x - 5 \rightarrow$

Add $1.5x$ to both sides: $5x - 17.5 < -5 \rightarrow$ Add 17.5 to both sides of the inequality.

$5x < 12.5 \rightarrow$ Divide both sides by 5. $\rightarrow \frac{5}{5}x < \frac{12.5}{5} \rightarrow x < 2.5$

25) Choice C is correct

$5(2x^6)^3 \Rightarrow 5 \times 2^3 \times x^{18} = 40x^{18}$

Effortless Math's ASVAB Online Center

... So Much More Online!

Effortless Math Online ASVAB Math Center offers a complete study program, including the following:

- ✓ Step-by-step instructions on how to prepare for the ASVAB Math test
- ✓ Numerous ASVAB Math worksheets to help you measure your math skills
- ✓ Complete list of ASVAB Math formulas
- ✓ Video lessons for ASVAB Math topics
- ✓ Full-length ASVAB Math practice tests
- ✓ And much more...

No Registration Required.

Visit **EffortlessMath.com/ASVAB** to find your online ASVAB Math resources.

Receive the PDF version of this book or get another FREE book!

Thank you for using our Book!

Do you LOVE this book?

Then, you can get the PDF version of this book or another book absolutely FREE!

Please email us at:

info@EffortlessMath.com

for details.

Author's Final Note

I hope you enjoyed reading this book. You've made it through the book! Great job!

First of all, thank you for purchasing this practice book. I know you could have picked any number of books to help you prepare for your ASVAB Math test, but you picked this book and for that I am extremely grateful.

It took me years to write this workbook for the ASVAB Math because I wanted to prepare a comprehensive ASVAB Math workbook to help test takers make the most effective use of their valuable time while preparing for the test.

After teaching and tutoring math courses for over a decade, I've gathered my personal notes and lessons to develop this practice book. It is my greatest hope that the exercises in this book could help you prepare for your test successfully.

If you have any questions, please contact me at reza@effortlessmath.com and I will be glad to assist. Your feedback will help me to greatly improve the quality of my books in the future and make this book even better. Furthermore, I expect that I have made a few minor errors somewhere in this book. If you think this to be the case, please let me know so I can fix the issue as soon as possible.

If you enjoyed this book and found some benefit in reading this, I'd like to hear from you and hope that you could take a quick minute to post a review on the book's Amazon page. To leave your valuable feedback, please visit: amzn.to/2ZXovn5

Or scan this QR code.

I personally go over every single review, to make sure my books really are reaching out and helping students and test takers. Please help me help ASVAB Math test takers, by leaving a review!

I wish you all the best in your future success!

Reza Nazari

Math teacher and author

Made in United States
Troutdale, OR
09/26/2023